The Rambles

of a

Wandering Priest

Allen Martin Bair

WestBow
PRESS
A DIVISION OF THOMAS NELSON

WestBow Press books may be ordered through booksellers or by contacting:
WestBow Press
A Division of Thomas Nelson
1663 Liberty Drive
Bloomington, IN 47403
www.westbowpress.com
1-(866) 928-1240

ISBN: 978-1-4497-3233-2 (sc)
ISBN: 978-1-4497-3235-6 (hc)
ISBN: 978-1-4497-3234-9 (e)
Library of Congress Control Number: 2011961170

Printed in the United States of America

WestBow Press rev. date: 11/29/2011

Contents

My Daily Prayer

Almighty Father, I confess and admit that I am poor, blind, weak, naked, and ignorant before You, and that I can do nothing of myself.

I ask that You would fill me with Your grace; that You would take full possession of these hands and these feet, this mouth, this heart, and this mind; that this person might be Jesus for people, give Jesus to people, receive Jesus from people, and see Jesus in people today.

I ask that You Yourself would overflow within me with Your presence and Your power, with Your love and Your compassion, with Your wisdom and Your humility, that others might come to know You through me, and that I might not say or do anything that You don't want me to say or do; and that I might say and do everything that You want me to say and do; that I might not cause harm or damage, and if I should that You would use that damage for good.

I thank You, I love You, I praise You, and I worship You, and I ask these things in the name of Jesus Christ my Lord. Amen.

The Priest Begins to Wander

There's a great line at the end of *The Bicentennial Man* in which the main character begins his address to the world congress with, "I have always tried to make sense of my life . . . " In many ways, that's the way I feel about my life, because on the surface, where sense is concerned, my life doesn't seem to make a whole lot of it.

When I began my journey, I was a non-denominational Christian from a Bible fellowship in Southern California. I then attended a non-denominational, anti-Catholic Bible school in Wisconsin, with the express intent of going on to become a missionary overseas in a remote tribal setting. At this point in my journey, I am an Old Catholic (similar to western rites Orthodox) priest living in northern Idaho with a commitment to minister to anyone the Lord brings my way. Along the way, I have been a part of or have attended Messianic Jewish, conservative Baptist, Pentecostal, Charismatic, Episcopal, Lutheran, United Church of Christ, Methodist, and Roman Catholic congregations, parishes, and churches. I have been in pastoral jobs, non-pastoral jobs, and jobs in which I did nothing but heavy lifting, pulling, grunting, and sweating all day long.

I began my journey pretty confident I knew what "real Christianity" was, what its doctrines looked like, and what they didn't look like. I thought I knew who was a Christian and who wasn't. I had devoted myself wholeheartedly to the Christianity and interpretation of Scripture that I had been taught, and to the denominational structure I had been taught by. I could tell you for certain which Bible you should use, what the real deal was on the end times, and which "churches" would lead you to hell.

I also began my journey with a disorder that hadn't even been recognized in the United States by the time I entered Bible school in my late teens, so I didn't know it had been impacting my life since infancy. I had always been socially awkward and inappropriate. When I was a kid, the psychologist said I had what was then called "hyperkinesis" (now called ADHD). From what I am told, he acknowledged that this diagnosis wasn't quite right, but that was all he could come up with at the time. It wouldn't be until much later, in my early thirties, that I would receive the correct diagnosis, Asperger's syndrome. This is a form of autism in which the person has a high degree of "academic" intelligence, but has a malfunction in the centers of the brain that process social, relational, and emotional information.

At the end of Bible school, just as I was on the very edge of pursuing my life's ambition of being an overseas missionary, my life got turned upside down and my goals lay in ruins. The organization to which I had dedicated myself had chosen to reject my application for practical missions training and instead chose to send me home to work more on my social difficulties. After a year of trying to do just this, my plans were utterly devastated when the pastors of my church refused to give me the reference I needed to return.

What followed was a journey that is still ongoing, as I began to be disabused of what I thought I knew about what it meant to be a Christian and what it meant to be a minister, a pastor, and a priest. Did I think a particular denomination was wrong? The Lord decided that was right where I needed to be. Did I decide that a particular book or philosophy was wrong? The Lord decided that was what I needed to read and understand from the author's perspective. All in all, the Lord decided to guide me in and out of all my preconceived ideas about who was right and who was wrong. He turned them on their heads without ever letting me actually stray from Him.

In the process of my journey, I have known more failure than I would ever care to experience again. I have also done things that are nearly miraculous for someone with my disorder. I have been happily married for thirteen years as of this writing, have three great kids, and I became a priest and have ministered more or less successfully by Grace to others in both traditional and non-traditional settings. I have also had the miracle of a good friend and psychiatrist not only confirming my disorder, but also treating it and normalizing what were previously abnormal brain patterns. The latter gave me the somewhat unique perspective I have today, which is the perspective I share in my rambles. Whatever else may happen in my life, or however many ways I may fail in everything else, I know that God has blessed me richly in these things.

Shortly after my biofeedback treatments, I began writing my rambles as notes I published on Facebook. I have been writing them in various places over a period of years as we've moved to different parts of the country. I had been writing my thoughts and viewpoints for years before I began posting on Facebook but had never before had a forum like the social media site to put them out there for others to read and give feedback. After a while, I began to get comments like, "You should start a blog." So I did, The *Wandering Priest*, which gets occasional hits. A little while later, several friends told me, "You should put your rambles into a book and get them published." This resulted in the book you now hold in your hands, which was possible only by the Grace and intervention of God through a generous donation from my dad.

The rambles are meant to start a discussion about things we don't want to talk about as Christians, especially as Christians in this modern age from different "opposing" denominations. They were meant to get people to begin thinking about and hopefully discussing what it really means to be Christian. The goal is to get us all talking to one another again, brother-to-brother and sister-to-sister, instead of Catholic to Protestant or Baptist to Charismatic. The rambles aren't meant to tell people which church or denomination they should belong to. While the rambles are obviously slanted towards Orthodoxy, my intent is to point people back to Jesus Christ Himself and for them to seek Him where they are.

This book is meant for self-professed Christians and is written primarily to self-professed Christians. I do not intend for it to be given to those who have not professed faith in Jesus Christ. They will misunderstand much of what I am talking about, because they don't have the experience needed for a common frame of reference.

One thing I want to make clear is why I refer to and directly quote *The Gospel of Buddha* by Paul Carus and *Tao Te Ching* by Lao Tzu. First, let me say that I am neither a Buddhist nor a Taoist, and I never will be. In the ancient Church, many Church Fathers borrowed freely from the philosophers and ideas of their day (stoicism, neo-Platonism, etc.) in order to complement their faith and understanding and enhance them. In my opinion, this is no different.

I learned from the teachings of the Buddha, Lao Tzu, Plato, and many others this important lesson: God may use anything and anyone to convey His truth, and that truth may be found buried in pagan philosophers, other religious writings, or even little green Jedi masters and R-rated films like *Matrix*. God is not limited to the boxes we try to stuff Him in, and He speaks to all who will listen in the way and language that they can understand. He doesn't want anyone to perish; He wants all to turn from their sins and come and follow Him.

Part I | Spiritual Autism

1 | A Ramble about Spiritual Autism

Developmental disorders are usually my wife's specialty. She has easily read enough literature on autism, fetal alcohol syndrome, mental retardation, and other disorders to qualify for any number of degrees on the subject (at least in my humble opinion). Autism, though, is one with which I have had to become far more familiar and intimate than I ever really wanted.

Autism is defined "by a characteristic triad of symptoms: impairments in social interaction; impairments in communication; and restricted interests and repetitive behavior" ("Autism", Wikipedia. org). It generally progresses from infancy into adulthood without remission and can so severely handicap a person as to appear similar to mental retardation. A related disorder within the autistic spectrum is called Asperger's syndrome. People with Asperger's syndrome also exhibit impairments in social interaction and communication, and they demonstrate obsessive behavior with limited interests. However, it differs with classical autism in that cognitive development and linguistic skills are generally not impaired but are actually often enhanced. People with Asperger's syndrome often possess a high academic intelligence, especially in logical or mechanical operations, but are bereft of any or most natural social skills, empathy, body language sensitivity, and emotional comprehension (depending on the severity and variance of the disorder within the individual person). A person with mild to moderate Asperger's syndrome can often function on his or her own and is able to somewhat "fit in" but is socially incapable and may appear to be rude or even arrogant without intending to. It is an extreme "left-brainedness".

Until recently, I was intimately familiar with Asperger's syndrome first-hand. Through a series of biofeedback treatments, a generous friend who is also a psychiatrist was able to jump-start those areas of my brain that were not functioning correctly. Two months ago was the first time I was able to process not only my own emotions but also the emotions and feelings of others in real time, without having to filter them through the logical reasoning part of my brain. I remember that, prior to this treatment, I was effectively alone no matter how many people surrounded me. All my attempts at understanding and relating to people were absolute failures. I was, essentially, emotionally locked into my own head with no means of escape, no means of freedom. The only way I could interact somewhat normally was by role-playing various social situations in my head and playing them back as those situations arose. The older I became, the better I got at it; but it still wasn't natural or normal, and it was exhausting for me. If I came into a situation for which I had no information on how to react . . . forget about it. My brain couldn't handle it. I hope you can imagine my gratitude to this man who has freed me from that social and relational blindness.

I've thought a lot about Asperger's syndrome since I began to suspect my condition a few years ago and even more since my diagnosis and treatments. I've come to believe that there is a parallel with the natural spiritual state of humanity. We are all suffering from a kind of spiritual autism or spiritual Asperger's syndrome.

I am speaking of course of what is referred to in theological circles as the sin nature, but the truth is that I don't like the word "sin" in describing it. First, because the word sin in English has been so abused, misused, and tainted with moralistic meaning that it really doesn't describe the problem. The word used in the Greek text of the New Testament is "hamartia." Literally, it means "disorder, malfunction, error, or mistake." Hamartia in Greek literature doesn't generally refer to a moral failing as such, but rather refers to a fatal flaw in the psyche of human beings that causes them to commit the wrongs which they try so desperately to avoid. A great example of this is the Greek play, Oedipus Rex, where King Oedipus, in his quest to morally avoid the atrocity he is prophesied to commit by killing his father and marrying his mother, falls into the trap of committing it anyway.

I believe what humanity has is much like autism. It is a genetically passed spiritual developmental disorder. Humanity is able to function cognitively quite highly, but when it comes to spiritually relating to God we have to role-play for the situation first and then call it back up when the situation arises. We cannot relate spiritually, or are at least deficient to various degrees in spiritual social skills. In my opinion, one of the ways we role-play in order to cope in a spiritual situation is by creating moral codes of conduct. What is actually called for is being able to empathize with, have compassion on, and be able to relate to God and other people on the spiritual level, but we can't do that by nature. So, just as a person with autism has to "fake" social skills in order to relate to those around him, we as human beings have to "fake" spiritual social skills. We then process the results of our role-playing through our own material and physical filters for use in later similar situations.

God, in His mercy, is like a parent with an autistic child when it comes to human beings. He is wholly and totally engaged with drawing the child out of his spiritually relational blindness. He wants the child to develop his communication skills with Him. He wants the child to recognize His presence, and He rejoices with any small progress the child makes, and works even harder at it when he regresses. The goal of God is for the child to experience normal communication with Him and with others, but it is fighting an uphill battle against a devastating disorder.

As I consider this in my own life I realize that reaching past the confines of my physical senses in order to recognize and experience Him is tremendously difficult. My own psyche is constantly bombarding me with physical sensory information that can't comprehend anything but these three dimensions. I think this is why God so often works within these three dimensions, using imagery and analogies from our own life experiences to help us to recognize Him and get to know Him.

Those of us who are baptized into Christ Jesus and His death are possessed of the Holy Spirit. He works tirelessly within us, much like the treatments that my friend gave me, to correct the disorder and get us to exercise our spiritual relational skills as far as we are able. But we must cooperate with His treatment, much like I had to cooperate with my friend's, and it is often frustrating and difficult as we are asked to trust something that we cannot comprehend.

The end result is this: If we cooperate with the Holy Spirit and move forward, then we will see progress and will experience our Father first hand in real time. If we don't cooperate, or don't begin the process by faith in Jesus Christ, we continue in our spiritual autism. And eventually, like a severely autistic person who isn't responding to treatment or to his parent's absolute devotion, we will have to be placed in a facility where we can do no harm to ourselves or to others, remaining locked in the suffering of our own desires, illusions, and fears. This isn't His desired outcome at all, and He wants us to be freed from it. Are we willing to cooperate with His treatments?

2 | A Ramble about Attachment Disorders

As part of my training for work I have to plow through a three-inch thick binder of reading materials. Most of it is a repeat of materials, laws, and regulations that I have already read or with which I have already become acquainted. But recently I read through a pamphlet in the binder on attachment disorders that caught my attention and got me thinking. It isn't the first time I have encountered material on Attachment Disorder (AD) or Reactive Attachment Disorder (RAD), but this time rusty gears started whirring.

In short, an attachment disorder occurs when a child fails, generally through either neglect or abuse, to form a healthy nurturing attachment to their parent. This in turn leads to an inability to form healthy attachments with other people as well, and can cause the child to either inappropriately cling to or completely reject and become abusive toward the people in his or her life. In many cases the child also becomes abusive toward themselves. The author of the article I read stated that such children will often try to cause their foster parents (assuming a foster care situation) to abuse them to try to get them to treat them as their abusive birth parents did. The author also states that such children engage in pathological lying, invent stories of being abused, and refuse to take responsibility for their actions, blaming others; such behavior continuing into adulthood.

I have previously referred to "sin" as a disorder or malfunction of the human psyche. The very word in Greek, hamartia, means "error, malfunction, disorder, mistake," and is used frequently in Greek literature to denote the "fatal flaw" which resides within every human being. I have also previously referred to it as a kind of spiritual autism or spiritual Asperger's syndrome where the person is initially unable to communicate or socialize normally with God or the spiritual world in general. I have also described the path of Jesus Christ as a kind of treatment plan for this disorder. Now I would like to explore these elements, add one or two more, and then try to put a bigger picture together.

Another psychologist, Abraham Maslow, described what he called a hierarchy of needs, also referred to as Maslow's pyramid. In it he describes five levels of need, each level of which must be realized and satisfied before the person can progress upwards: 1) physiological, 2) safety and security, 3) love/belonging, 4) esteem, 5) self-actualization. This scheme is debated as to which level should go where, and that it doesn't always look the same in every individual, but the basic idea is sound. It is when a need is perceived as not being met that psychological aberrations begin to occur, and the person is often unable to progress to the next level.

Another piece of the puzzle I am attempting to put together lies in the descriptions given of experiences of deep prayer, meditation, and even enlightenment among the various mystical traditions. To condense what a great number of such witnesses say: when one draws ever closer to God to the point where there is only the individual and God, and the lines begin to blur, the general consensus of those witnesses is the experience of overwhelming peace, joy, love, and fulfillment in knowing Him in an intimate way.

I would posit that the human being's "natural" state was to be in a constant intimate relationship with God. Such a relationship would consistently and permanently meet all that person's needs for safety, love, belonging, esteem, and self-actualization. It would not matter if everything collapsed and burned down around them (as has also been reported as being experienced); this constant relationship and awareness would continuously ensure that those needs would be met. I should add here that in this kind of relationship it would also be understood that the physical needs, while important, would likely be considered of secondary importance (also reported as being experienced).

The hamartia disorder renders the human being unable to communicate or relate normally with God. Like a person with Asperger's or autism, the person is often aware of God, or rather aware of the absence of "Something," but is unable to socialize normally or experience normal relationship. It is not that God is not present, but that the person in question is unable to recognize that presence without promptings from Him, and often even with promptings the person is unable to recognize and respond appropriately to Him.

This leads to the perception that somehow God, the Primary Parent, is not present or is somehow neglectful of the person, whether or not that is the actual reality. This then precipitates a kind of attachment disorder with God. More often then not, because of the initial disorder, our perception of God is all too often a misperception or a fantasy created in our mind of what we expect God to be because of our lack of direct experience or "observation." The mind creates an image to which it then attaches the label "God" with God Himself being formless and imageless. We lie, we refuse to take responsibility, we become abusive to ourselves, to our perception of God, and to other people. We cling to our perceptions or fantasies about God, or we reject them outright hoping that He will love us while we tell Him how much we hate Him.

This also lends itself to the conclusion that it is this primary disorder, hamartia, which is the root cause of all other disorders. Without the psyche's uninterrupted relationship with God from birth, the psyche then turns to the people around itself to fulfill those needs perceived as being unfulfilled. This then leads to a Russian roulette where the person's apparent psychological health is dependent largely on the circumstances of his birth, childhood, and upraising, as well as his own choices which are highly influenced by these factors.

Even after a person is baptized, and is so joined to God through being grafted onto Christ, there is still the matter of integrating that new state. The person has developed a lifetime of behaviors that were developed while unable to respond to the presence of God, and now they must integrate that new sense and ability into their pattern of behavior, which takes both time and practice. Integration does not happen immediately, and it must progress before the full benefits of such treatment can be realized, at least in this life.

It stands to reason that we will relate to God in the same way that we relate to other people. If we present a false front to other people, we will likely attempt to do so with God. If we are honest with other people and open, we are likely to be honest and open with God. If we are capable of dysfunctional relationships with other people, then we are equally capable of it with God and are likely to treat Him thus.

In spite of all this, God is still present. He still loves us. He still wants desperately for us to work through this and to know Him, knowing the whole time the kind of fight and struggle it will be. He wants us to succeed in this and ultimately to experience deep, intimate, normal relationship with Him. The way things were supposed to be.

3 | A Ramble about Temptation

The Scriptures say,

Let no one say when he is tempted, "I am being tempted by God," for God cannot be tempted with evil, and he himself tempts no one. But each person is tempted when he is lured and enticed by his own desire. Then desire when it has conceived gives birth to sin, and sin when it is fully grown brings forth death. (James 1:13-15, WEB)

Temptations occur because inwardly we want something (or don't want something, as the case may be), and are then told, "No, you can't have it your way." For example, someone who absolutely cannot stand chocolate will not be tempted to eat it even if a hundred bars of chocolate are placed in front of him. This must be understood and accepted: if you are tempted to do something, it is because somewhere within you is the desire to do it.

We don't like to admit that fact. The married man who believes himself to be godly may refuse to admit to himself that he struggles with adulterous thoughts because he is somehow sexually attracted to women other than his wife. In other words, he doesn't want to admit that he is capable of such a thing, when in fact deep down he is not only perfectly capable of it, but a part of him wants to do so.

The fact that the temptation occurs is a glaring reminder of our deep spiritual disorder; a disorder we may pay lip service to, but is painful to be reminded of in reality. It is so disturbing and traumatic to the human psyche to be faced with this disorder that a person's mind can throw everything possible at him in order to avoid dealing with the reality of it.

This is why God permits temptations. We have a deep need to be constantly reminded of our problem because we, by nature, constantly seek to ignore it and remain in self-denial about it. We have to be shown this on a regular basis. If we aren't, we will fall into the delusion that there's nothing wrong with us. Our salvation depends on us drawing nearer to God through Jesus Christ. Without the constant reminder of the problem, most of us (myself included), would drift farther and farther away as we delude ourselves into thinking that we don't have a problem and so don't need to approach Him in prayer and confession.

As 1 Corinthians 10:13 says, God allows the temptation to go so far, but no farther. The purpose behind permitting them is therapeutic; it is not to make us slide farther into the abyss. They are intended to be just enough to remind us of our spiritual disorder and our need for Him. They are not intended to be enough to where we can't say, "No." He does not intend that we be sent spiraling downwards beyond our control.

If we are tempted to eat doughnuts when on a diet, it is because we want to eat the doughnuts and have been told no. If we are tempted to steal, it is because we want the item in question, and feel that we have every right to violate the person from whom we are taking it. If we are tempted to "sexual misconduct," it is because we are sexually aroused by the thought of it and want to do it. It is not the fault of the bikini-clad girl that the self-professed Christian man struggles with his thoughts about her. The man desires her, refuses to admit it to himself or God, and continues to struggle in a losing battle until he does admit it and seeks help. Making her put on a tee shirt and blaming her for her indiscretion doesn't remove the primary problem within the man. It might be kind of her to do so in recognition of the man's weakness, but it is the man's weakness that is the issue, not her choice of swimwear.

The ironic thing about the above example is that we, as Christian men, have a tendency to become angry with the woman and blame her rather than facing the problem within ourselves. There are some men who will blame the woman for being raped if the clothing she wore was too provocative. There are many thieves who will blame the person they stole from for their thievery. There are many people who eat doughnuts who blame the baker for making them.

The first step in the treatment of any disorder or addiction is admitting that you have one. Once this is done, in order to continue making progress you must continuously be aware that you still have that problem and come to terms with it on a regular basis. It isn't the liquor store's fault if a recovering alcoholic walks in and buys the alcohol believing that he no longer has that problem. For all intents and purposes, it isn't the drug dealer's fault if the recovering addict pops by on the street corner for a quick fix because he thinks he can handle it. If I myself were to pop by and speak to the same dealer there would be no issue because I myself have no such addiction and would not be tempted to buy and use it.

Removing the temptation only serves to delay the inevitable if the root problem is not faced and admitted. I love watching Stargate. It is also a distraction from spiritual pursuits. Putting away the DVDs for a while doesn't solve the problem, it only delays it. Removing the DVDs altogether doesn't solve the problem, because I will be tempted to go out and replace them. The root problem is the desire to escape from reality by watching Stargate and seeing "what happens next."

In some respects, that God permits temptation can be one of His greatest gifts in our spiritual growth because it encourages us to keep our eyes focused on Him, where they need to be, and to face the reality of our spiritual disorder.

4 | A Ramble about Confessions

As a part of my job as a residential care worker, I get to participate in various "groups" held by the residents. In one of these groups the kids get together for the express purpose of admitting to things they have done. They choose these things from among one or more of nine problems written on a list, such as a problem with authority for example. Sometimes these problems are called up because we, as staff, have given them paperwork to fill out because we see the problem being displayed. Sometimes they see the problem themselves and address it. Other times their peers call out their problems for them, and the person either acknowledges it or says they will "look into it."

I have sat through many of these groups now. And there are two things that strike me most about them. The first is how much like the sacrament of confession they are in intent. The second is, like many confessions, how phony many of these admittals are. The hypocrisy is overwhelming at times. The only reason why these kids usually call them out and admit them is because they're required to or they lose the ability to do anything fun. Ideally, the kids that have been there longer are supposed to guide the newer kids in how to explore and call out their problems. In reality, they only show them how to give the mechanical responses everyone expects.

There's no sincerity. There's no real change of heart. It's so mechanical that the kids read through the list of problems at such breakneck speed that I usually can't understand what they're saying, and many don't even bother to actually read through the list. They just read off the number or letter of the point on the outline. They get extremely annoyed when I ask them to slow down their reading. After the groups are done, they will frequently behave in such a way so as to receive more paperwork for the very same things that they just admitted they recognized as a problem, and the cycle will repeat itself.

I do a lot of listening to the kids, too. Often I let them talk about more then they are supposed to be allowed to in order to determine where they're really at from day to day. From these conversations it's pretty easy to see that very little has changed even after the groups. The behavior of those kids who have been there longer may have changed to conform to the standards so that they don't get into as much trouble, but the beliefs and attitudes which caused the initial behavior seem just as prevalent. They fall into line just enough to merit discharge, but intend on falling back into the same things that precipitated the need for them to be in the facility they're in.

I can't help but think when I am at work how much like the Church this is. How often do we go to confession (whether with a priest, in a church service, or in private) just going through the routine and asking forgiveness with no real intent of changing the causes within our hearts which precipitated the need for confession to begin with? We only go through the motions in order to get out of any disciplinary action, and then like the kids I work with, we are mechanically told "good job for calling your problems" by our peers.

Do we really think we're fooling God into thinking we are actually repentant? If I, as a human staff member, am able to see through the false fronts, how much more does God see into our hearts knowing what our true intent is?

In the same way that the purpose of the groups is bringing the kids back into the normal practice of the program, the purpose of Confession is to reconcile us to God and to each other. It is to recognize our change of mind and heart, and to bring us back into communion with each other and with God. It is to acknowledge our failures and reach out for help in moving past them. Simply saying what we did wrong and expecting an absolution so that we don't have to face discipline is a misuse and abuse of the program, and of the practice of Confession, and is a deep misunderstanding of both.

I can't say that I am any different because I am equally guilty of this. How many times have I gone to the Lord mechanically only because somewhere in the back of my mind I think I will somehow escape discipline or consequences for what I have thought, said, or done; all the while not letting go of the passions, fears, or desires which were the causes of what I have thought, said, or done?

God sees all of it, and we can hide nothing from Him. He sees more about us than we do. He also knows when we're faking it just to be perceived as advancing in the program.

5 | On Loving God

The greatest commandment is, "You will love the Lord your God with all your heart, with all you soul, with all your strength and with all your mind." There is no commandment in Holy Scripture more important than this one.

It is also impossible.

Because of our sin disorder, we are incapable of it. As hard as we may try, it is impossible to keep. The only person who can keep this command is God Himself.

St. John writes, "We love Him because He first loved us." God the Son must love God the Father through us, and this kind of love is initiated only by the Grace that is given by God. It cannot be forced, initiated, or earned by us.

In order for any action to be meaningful in this capacity it must be initiated and powered by Grace. Love for God is no exception. We must beg Him for the Grace to love Him as we ought, and be patient as He waits for the right time to bestow it. Too soon, and it could lead to our downfall through pride.

We must ask Him in all sincerity for even the ability to fulfill this most important and most basic commandment. We won't be able to fulfill it until we do, and it won't come until He deems us ready for it. It won't come until we discover the further depth of our inability and disorder, also by Grace.

It is frustrating and humiliating, but also necessary that this ability isn't given in the way we would wish right away. Otherwise much good may be lost, and God knows better than that.

Part II | Faith, Prosperity, and Possessions

1 | A Ramble about Money

I recently heard from another pastor friend of mine who is starting a study series about money and finances. It's not really a bad topic. Truth is, I'm horrible at keeping track of my own finances and anyone who knows me knows this is true. But for some reason, it just doesn't strike a very good chord in me to be talking about money at what is essentially supposed to be a meeting that teaches more about what it means to follow Jesus Christ.

I had the same reaction recently from a church newsletter I got. This particular church is usually very careful about when it mentions the offering and takes great pains to not even pass around the collection plate, preferring anonymous donations dropped in the box in the back. But lately, because of the economic crisis that has been hitting everyone, they've had to start mentioning it a little more often. Pastors still need to eat, and rent still needs to be paid. I really can't criticize this. I know firsthand what it means to draw your living from a church offering, and what that living often amounts to when all you see is five or ten dollars here or there. It's disheartening, frustrating, and difficult.

It is my observation that many good pastors really don't want to talk about money, but find themselves forced to. It becomes a necessary evil just to keep the church's lights on, and to keep gas in their car so they can make it to church. The Bible itself several times indicates that the worker is worthy of his (or her) wages, and that those who preach the gospel should live by the gospel. It becomes incredibly difficult to maintain one's credibility as a servant of God and a follower of Jesus Christ, who taught us not to worry about what we should eat or what we should wear, to then have to go to their congregations and ask to be paid a living wage. It's really not fair, because there seems to be a number of "pastors" who have no real issues with this and live lives some heads of state can only fantasize about.

Money tends to turn the Church of Jesus Christ into a business. Some denominations even go so far as to have their members sign what is effectively a legal document; a pledge to give so much money per month so they can know what their balance sheet is going to look like. Many Seminaries now teach more business administration than pastoring for this reason.

In the gospels and in the book of Acts we see Jesus having taught a very different view and practice of money than the one we are taught almost from birth as Americans (in particular). Jesus taught His first disciples to give up everything and follow Him. From what can be seen from the Scriptures, the first disciples literally left everything and traveled, homeless, with Jesus. Their income came from a group of women who provided for them out of their own pockets, and when they had nothing, there is no record that Jesus ever told them to solicit the people for anything. When He sent them out, He sent them out with the explicit instruction that they were to take only the clothes on their backs. He told them not to worry about what they would eat or wear or drink, but to put first the Kingdom of Heaven, and then all of these things would be given to them. In the Scriptures Peter says very clearly that they had left everything to follow Him, and when Jesus called men to follow Him, the explicit or implicit instruction was to leave everything else behind, or to sell it and give it to the poor.

In the Book of Acts, we see the Apostles and other disciples carrying out the same manner of living and teaching as everyone who was added to the Church went and sold everything they had, and then brought the money to the Apostles. The Apostles then distributed money and food to everyone in the Church as it was needed, so no one went without. When some prejudice or abuses began, the Apostles set Deacons over the whole process to police it. Notice also in Acts that this process was voluntary. It wasn't a requirement of membership. People gave according to what faith they possessed that God would provide for them, and that faith, as much or as little as they possessed, was received and welcomed, and they were not belittled or asked for more. The only record where it was called into question has to do with a couple attempting to deceive God, the Apostles, the Church, and themselves. God Himself through Peter met this deception, not their lack of faith, with grave consequences.

We don't do this today. Why? I know for myself, I would be scared to give everything I had to a church's leadership if I didn't know I could trust them or the mechanism in place to ensure that me and mine were taken care of. I would be scared of the inevitable church politics and people who might slight me or mine or somehow make it so that we went hungry. And of course there is the attachment to things (something Jesus Christ taught not to do by the way), and how am I to acquire those pleasant toys and luxuries for myself without money of my own? And then there is the fact that we call this form of economy "Communism" or "Socialism" in this day and age. Neither word sits well with most Americans, and both words stir up a patriotic backlash and promotion of capitalism and a free market economy. Jesus Christ, with what he taught, would be labeled a liberal communist by many in the conservative community; except of course that most of these profess to follow Him, and so conveniently gloss over and theologically sanitize this part of His teaching.

If we are going to profess to follow Jesus Christ, then we need to actually follow Him and what he taught. The truth is that in the state that our economy and the world's economy find themselves in, what Jesus taught and the Apostles practiced would be more relevant for the Church today than at almost any other point in our history. If we all pooled our resources into a single fund and then doled out to everyone as needs required within the Church, chances are no one would go hungry, have their bills unpaid, or have to worry about their rent. The rest of the world would crash down around their ears, but they would be unmoved economically and would be financially secured.

It would require following the principles of detachment from material things, and trust in God's provision as Jesus Christ taught. It would require a radical revamp of the Church as we know it. Are we willing to put our money where our mouth is and follow Him?

2 | A Ramble about Prosperity

There was a Saint in the ancient Church who said that God had ordained that everything which is truly needful and necessary for spiritual growth, progressing in our prayer, and knowing God; everything which we need to move from sinner to saint God has given to us freely and in abundance: poverty, solitude, hard work, tears, prayer, Grace, and more. But he also said those things which hinder our spiritual growth and obstruct our prayer, that can throw us off and lead us away from him, these things God has made very difficult to obtain: money, comfort, ease, security, and so on. He said you actually have to work very hard to obtain the things which will poison your relationship with God, while you practically have to do nothing at all to receive the things which can strengthen it.

"But God wants me to be rich!" This seems to be the battle cry, and the main message, of a great many preachers and pastors today. Their "churches" look much more like concert halls, and their congregations number in the tens of thousands. Their sermons often sound more like financial seminars aimed at helping people achieve financial security, personal wealth, and independence. They write book after book teaching people how to feel better about themselves, how to acquire more possessions, and how to satisfy themselves, and they do so all because "God wants me to be happy."

God loves us dearly. There is no question about that. But like a good parent, He wants what is best for His children. He wants them to be healthy, mature properly, have a good education, and enjoy the best He has to give. He also wants to keep them away from anything that can harm them. This includes anything which can become an addiction or poison, and those things which can ruin their relationship with Him. In short, like any good parent, He doesn't want us to do anything that could harm us.

And like most children, we have no real idea what is actually best for us. We want what feels good to us. We want the candy. We want the toys and more of them. We want to be first in everything. If we get a cut we want Him to put a Band-Aid on it and make it better even if we got it doing what He told us not to do. And we throw temper tantrums when we ask Him for something, and He says, "No."

Jesus didn't go around teaching people how to play the stock market, or how to be financially successful. When someone asked to follow Him, He told him to sell everything he had, give the money to the homeless and then come and follow Him. The New Testament is very clear about Jesus' own financial state. He was homeless, and He and His disciples were provided for by the financial means of a few women. After Pentecost, it was a regular practice of the Church for its members to sell any property they had and give the proceeds to the Apostles, who then distributed the money to anyone who needed it. In the writings of the Fathers, voluntary poverty is always encouraged for Christians to follow as the preferred financial state.

One of these Fathers, Evagrios the Solitary (4th century), wrote passionately about this. He said that the "demon" of avarice is particularly deceitful because it will come in pretending to be concerned about the poor, and then suggest to you that you need to somehow acquire more money and more income so that you can help the poor. But then once you start focusing on that, it turns your mind away from Christ and on to the matters of acquiring more and more money, and thus the downward spiral continues until you are Christian in name only, and eventually, even this is lost. These Fathers taught to give until you had nothing left, and were poor yourself.

This "prosperity gospel" teaching is nothing short of a demonic heresy designed to pull people away from Jesus Christ, not bring them towards Him. It profoundly contradicts both the teaching and example of our Lord, and perversely does so in His name. It throws the gates of avarice, gluttony, and self-esteem wide open for all the demonic passions to run through and paints a smiley face with a cross on them. It is a trap which leads not to Eternal Life, but a curt "I'm sorry, who are you?" from our Lord.

Having possessions isn't wrong. It's letting those possessions control you. Having money isn't wrong, it's letting the desire for money control you. Very few people in this world are able to have a lot of "stuff" without letting that "stuff" control them. Jesus Himself said that it was easier for a camel to go through the eye of a sewing needle than it was for a rich man to enter the Kingdom of God. The vast majority of us really can't handle it that well, at least if we were truly honest with ourselves.

God gives His good gifts freely. But like the child looking at the plate of broccoli, we don't always see it that way. We want the bag of candy, and to heck with the stomachache and vomiting to follow!

3 | A Ramble about the Middle Path

I recently read a pamphlet I received from a church I visited that says, "Moderation: We believe the experience and daily walk of the believer should never lead him into extremes of fanaticism." I find it intriguing that this same church also disseminated a pamphlet, written by the pastor of that church, about how regular and cheerful tithing was just as important as Holy Communion in God's redemptive plan, and was the key to wealth, promotions, higher positions, etc.

Moderation can be defined as "not too much, and not too little." It is somewhere in the middle between extremes. It can also be called the Middle Path. Immoderation, going to extremes of either too much or too little can be harmful in many, many things. The person who comes to my mind in speaking about moderation, or "the Middle Path," is Gautama Siddharta, or the Buddha.

The Buddha, Gautama Siddharta, said,

"The Tathagata [lit. "the Perfect One"] . . . does not seek salvation in austerities, but neither does he for that reason indulge in worldly pleasures, nor live in abundance. The Tathagata has found the middle path.

"There are two extremes, O bhikkus [lit. "disciples"], which the man who has given up the world ought not to follow—the habitual practice, on the one hand, of self-indulgence which is unworthy, vain and fit only for the worldly minded—and the habitual practice, on the other hand, of self-mortification, which is painful, useless and unprofitable.

"Neither abstinence from fish and flesh, nor going naked, nor shaving the head, nor wearing matted hair, nor dressing in a rough garment, nor covering oneself with dirt, nor sacrificing to Agni, will cleanse a man who is not free from delusions. Reading the Vedas, making offerings to priests, or sacrifices to the gods, self-mortification by heat or cold, and many such penances performed for the sake of immortality, these do not cleanse the man who is not free from delusions. Anger, drunkenness, obstinacy, bigotry, deception, envy, self-praise, disparaging others, superciliousness and evil intentions constitute uncleanness; not verily the eating of flesh.

"A middle path, O bhikkhus, avoiding the two extremes, has been discovered by the Tathagata—a path which opens the eyes, and bestows understanding, which leads to peace of mind, to the higher wisdom, to full enlightenment, to Nirvana! . . . By suffering, the emaciated devotee produces confusion and sickly thoughts in his mind. Mortification is not conducive even to worldly knowledge; how much less to a triumph over the senses! . . .

"And how can any one be free from self by leading a wretched life, if he does not succeed in quenching the fires of lust, if he still hankers after either worldly or heavenly pleasures? But he in whom self has become extinct is free from lust; he will desire neither worldly nor heavenly pleasures, and the satisfaction of his natural wants will not defile him. However, let him be moderate, let him eat and drink according to the need of the body.

"Sensuality is enervating; the self-indulgent man is a slave to his passions, and pleasure-seeking is degrading and vulgar. But to satisfy the necessities of life is not evil. To keep the body in good health is a duty, for otherwise we shall not be able to trim the lamp of wisdom, and keep our minds strong and clear. Water surrounds the lotus-flower, but does not wet its petals. This is the middle path,

O bhikkhus, that keeps aloof from both extremes." ("Gospel of Buddha," Paul Carus)

In another place, he talks about his experience hearing a musician teaching his apprentice how to tune a stringed instrument. If you make the string too tight, it will snap, and if you make it too loose, it will not play. You have to find the right point in between the two opposite extremes or the instrument simply will not play right, if at all. I've watched my wife tune her guitar several times. I've also heard her guitar when it's not tuned. Often she has to use an electronic tuner to tell her when a string is in tune and when it isn't, because she can't always discern it by ear. But it is very apparent when she tries to play it.

The Middle Path is the point between all opposite extremes. If you can imagine a number line, in one direction it heads off into the positive numbers 1, 2, 3, 4, etc. stretching into infinity. In the other direction it heads off into the negative numbers -1, -2, -3, -4, etc. stretching into infinity. Right in the middle between these two infinities lies the number "0". It is the inverse image of infinity and the only other number that shares many of the mathematical properties of infinity without being infinity. Furthermore, any deviation from zero results in a spiral towards either infinite accumulation or infinite debt. The Middle Path is like zero. It is the only point in between either extreme that doesn't lead to excesses. It is the zero point. The still point. The point at which all action or reaction, all motion, ceases. This brings to mind God, who is Himself motionless and stationary in reference to both time and space which pass through Him.

"Be still and know that I am God." However often this saying from the Psalms is taken out of context by New-Agers, there is a timeless truth and instruction for us about the Middle Path. To be still is to rest from all motion. We are creatures of motion. It is in our nature to move because we move naturally through time and space. But God "as He is" is the opposite. We move through Him and encounter His involvement in our lives through our natural motion in time and space, but to draw closer to Him as He is, we must draw back and be still. We must counter our natural instinct to move and act with non-motion. It is not doing nothing, but it is a deliberate and concentrated effort to keep from engaging in actions which would begin our spiral to the right hand or to the left, towards infinite debt or infinite accumulation. It is keeping from engaging in anything which would distract us from Him, the One who does not change, because change implies motion and vice versa.

Seeking to acquire more wealth, a better job, to achieve greater self-esteem; this is all motion. It draws us away from the center, the Middle, the Zero Point. Engaging in sensual pleasure of any kind is motion. In the same way, starving yourself, beating yourself, going to extremes to punish yourself, this is also motion. It is motion in the opposite direction, but it is still motion. Anything we do with our self or selfish interests as the cause is motion away from the Middle.

More than anyone else, we who profess to follow Jesus Christ should be seeking the Middle Path, the point between all opposite extremes. We should be ready to use and be thankful for what God gives, but not cling to it and seek to acquire more. We should take care of our bodies as though we were caring for a broken arm or a wound we are trying to get to heal, but we should not let our bodies' desires consume us and distract us from our goal. As Jesus taught, we should cut off every addiction which tempts us away from the Eternal Life which is union with God Himself, even as we must still live until God says otherwise.

The Path of Jesus Christ walks a fine, razor sharp line that if we go to the right or the left we step off the path. We know when we are in the Middle, at the Zero Point, when we cease from motion towards ourselves, be it positive or negative.

4 | A Ramble about Needs

Several years ago, I was a part of a short-term missions program/college course in Papua New Guinea. I spent two months in New Guinea. Most of that time was spent on the bamboo hut campus situated up in the Bena Bena tribe in the highlands, but there were a few excursions out to other existing mission sites. One of these excursions was an overnight to the Yagaria tribe, also located in the highlands a few hours drive from the campus.

Another student and I spent the night in the home of one of the Christian men from that tribe. His name was Michael. He and his family lived in what can loosely be described as a two-bedroom bamboo, wood, and "pit-pit" hut, raised off the ground. He kept his chickens and pigs underneath his house. Just outside his house, but within a fence, was his large garden where he grew most of their food. He and his family were barefoot, as most rural New Guineans were. They cooked their meals over a fire pit started in the traditional way, which involved bamboo, wood, and a lot of friction. As my companion and I shared a meal with our host, we talked with him. His English wasn't great, but then neither was our Pidgin (one of the things we spent our time learning on campus). Between our bad

31

Pidgin and his bad English we managed to eke out a conversation of sorts. It is a conversation that I still remember almost eighteen years later.

The thing I remember most about that conversation was when he said something to the effect of, "You Americans have all this money, bajillions and zillions of dollars, and you come here, and you aren't happy. Look at me, all I have is my family, my home, and my garden, and we're happy. We have everything we need."

I spent those two months that summer possessing only what I brought with me and could keep in my cabin. I remember when I returned to the US, and to my bedroom full of stuff, I was in a kind of shock. Reverse culture shock is normal for this kind of thing, but I distinctly remember looking around my bedroom and realizing how many things I had that I didn't actually need. I knew I didn't need it because I had just gone for two months without it and survived just fine.

It doesn't seem to make any difference anymore how much money you have or make, it never seems to be enough. When my wife and I were first married, we would have been thrilled to be making $35,000 a year. Somewhere in our minds, we thought, "If only we were able to make this amount of money, then we'll be ok." When we were living in California, we were making a little over $36,000 and we were barely scraping by. It never seemed to be enough. I have a friend who was making something like $95,000 per year, and as he described it to me, he said something like, "Even with that kind of money, we were barely keeping our heads above water."

When we have money or possessions, it always seems like we never have enough. We always think we need more, or we find a reason why we need more. Near as I can tell, this is the reason for the debt that my family and I are in right now. Some of those things we went into debt to get were things we really did need at the time. Some of them seemed a lot like needs at the time. Thinking back, I wonder if they really were, but hindsight is always at least 20/20.

Evagrios the Solitary, one of the Fathers of the Christian contemplative tradition, along with other writers, gave what I think is very sound advice for the Christian, although it is very difficult to practice living among the rest of the world. He said, in a nutshell, don't own anything and what you have give away. Even if you desire to have more money to be able to give it to the poor, this is only a trap laid for you by the enemy to get you to give in to thinly disguised avarice, the desire to have more. And once you give in to avarice, you open the doorway for other demons (literal or figurative) to rush in and attack. He and the others taught that it is completely possible to carry out the teachings of Christ if you own nothing. They also taught that it can be a hindrance to those teachings if you do own something, and especially if you seek to own something, regardless of the justification for it. What's most important is that they not only taught it, but they put what they taught into practice as well.

The more I keep this in mind, the more I realize how infested with this avarice I have become. I seek and desire things that, truthfully, I just don't need. I want them just to have them. I justify this in my mind by something like, "Well, what if I need it at some point in time and don't have it?" It doesn't matter if it's books, games, or programs, or whether they are paid or free.

I haven't thought about Michael from the Yagaria for a long time, but I never forgot him or his family. Somehow, somewhere they've always been in the back of my mind. Thinking back, I wish they had been in the forefront a little more.

5 | A Ramble about Living by Faith

The concept of living by faith seems to be badly misunderstood. It is all too often misinterpreted as something radically ungodly and unchristian, refusing to work and somehow expecting other people to provide for you. For this reason, it seems like people take one of the two extremes; either they do just that, and refuse to work, or they reject the notion altogether and depend heavily on their own jobs and what they can earn with their own hands. Neither are what the Scriptures or Sacred Tradition teach.

The truth is that how we live and what we depend on for our physical needs is no different from what we depend on for our spiritual needs. The physical aspect of our lives is no less subject to the necessity of cooperation with the Grace of God than the spiritual aspect if we are to follow the path of Jesus Christ. We depend on the Grace of God, by faith, that God will transform us into the image of Christ if we cooperate with Him. We must also depend on Him, by faith, in the same way for the things we need to live in this world, cooperating with His Grace.

The Holy Scriptures say this:

"Don't lay up treasures for yourselves on the earth, where moth and rust consume, and where thieves break through and steal; but lay up for yourselves treasures in heaven, where neither moth nor rust consume, and where thieves don't break through and steal; for where your treasure is, there your heart will be also. The lamp of the body is the eye. If therefore your eye is sound, your whole body will be full of light. But if your eye is evil, your whole body will be full of darkness. If therefore the light that is in you is darkness, how great is the darkness! No one can serve two masters, for either he will hate the one and love the other; or else he will be devoted to one and despise the other. You can't serve both God and Mammon. Therefore, I tell you, don't be anxious for your life: what you will eat, or what you will drink; nor yet for your body, what you will wear. Isn't life more than food, and the body more than clothing? See the birds of the sky, that they don't sow, neither do they reap, nor gather into barns. Your heavenly Father feeds them. Aren't you of much more value than they? Which of you, by being anxious, can add one moment to his lifespan? Why are you anxious about clothing? Consider the lilies of the field, how they grow. They don't toil, neither do they spin, yet I tell you that even Solomon in all his glory was not dressed like one of these. But if God so clothes the grass of the field, which today exists, and tomorrow is thrown into the oven, won't he much more clothe you, you of little faith? Therefore don't be anxious, saying, 'What will we eat?', 'What will we drink?' or, 'With what will we be clothed?' For the Gentiles seek after all these things; for your heavenly Father knows that you need all these things. But seek first God's Kingdom, and his righteousness; and all these things will be given to you as well. Therefore don't be anxious for tomorrow, for tomorrow will be anxious for itself. Each day's own evil is sufficient. (Matthew 6:19-34, WEB)

And this:

One of the multitude said to him, "Teacher, tell my brother to divide the inheritance with me." But he said to him, "Man, who made me a judge or an arbitrator over you?" He said to them, "Beware! Keep yourselves from covetousness, for a man's life doesn't consist of the abundance of the things which he possesses." He spoke a parable to them, saying, "The ground of a certain rich man brought forth abundantly. He reasoned within himself, saying, 'What will I do, because I don't have room to store my crops?' He said, 'This is what I will do. I will pull down my barns, and build bigger ones, and there I will store all my grain and my goods. I will tell my soul, "Soul, you have many goods laid up for many years. Take your ease, eat, drink, be merry."'" "But God said to him, 'You foolish one, tonight your soul is required of you. The things which you have prepared—whose will they be?' So is he who lays up treasure for himself, and is not rich toward God." He said to his disciples, "Therefore I tell you, don't be anxious for your life, what you will eat, nor yet for your body, what you will wear. Life is more than food, and the body is more than clothing. Consider the ravens: they don't sow, they don't reap, they have no warehouse or barn, and God feeds them. How much more valuable are you than birds! Which of you by being anxious can add a cubit to his height? If then you aren't able to do even the least things, why are you anxious about the rest? Consider the lilies, how they grow. They don't toil, neither do they spin; yet I tell you, even Solomon in all his glory was not arrayed like one of these. But if this is how God clothes the grass in the field, which today exists, and tomorrow is cast into the oven, how much more will he clothe you, O you of little faith? Don't seek what you will eat or what you will drink; neither be anxious. For the nations of the world seek after all of these things, but your Father knows that you need these things. But seek God's Kingdom, and all these things will be added to you. Don't be afraid, little flock, for it is your Father's good pleasure to give you the Kingdom. Sell that which you have, and give gifts to the needy. Make for yourselves purses which don't grow old, a treasure in the heavens that doesn't fail, where no thief approaches, neither moth destroys. For where your treasure is, there will your heart be also. (Luke 12:13-34, WEB)

What critics of living by faith don't tend to understand is that we live by faith whether we're aware of it or not. What Jesus was pointing out was not whether we are to live by faith, we do that anyway, but what our faith is in. What He was saying is, firstly, if you are putting your faith in your own ability to provide for yourself, you are a fool because you don't know what will happen from one day to the next. Secondly, He was speaking against avarice, which itself is often born out of the fear that you won't have enough from day to day.

Living by faith means understanding that it is God who provides all of our needs, regardless of what physical source they come from. Whether your needs are provided through an employer who pays you for the work you do, or if they come from a friend who wants to help, or if they come gift-wrapped in a basket left on your doorstep by some birds who happened your way, it is ultimately God who provides the employment, the friend, and the helpful basket-weaving birds. This should be more apparent in the economy today as so many people find out that it isn't by their efforts and abilities alone that they have jobs to go to, but by the mercy of God. Having your job today doesn't guarantee that you will have one tomorrow in which to place your trust.

But in the same way as having a job that God provides for you, living by faith requires that you cooperate with God in it. When you have an employer, it requires that you do the work your employer asks you to do. When you aren't deriving a paycheck by that means, it requires that you do the work that God has set up for you to do at the moment. When God provides food for the birds, it is true that they neither sow or reap, but they still have to get down low enough to hunt small animals, or gather seed. If they choose not to do this, they will starve even if surrounded by food.

There are some jobs that God tells people to do that preclude them from drawing a paycheck in the normal fashion because they legitimately can't do both without both suffering. This doesn't mean they don't work, but it does mean that they don't get paid for the work they do. In this case they must rely on their faith that God will provide for their needs by other means. There are some times, like the present day, when jobs are scarce to be had. Does this mean that God abandons His people? Does it mean He causes His rain to stop falling on either the faithful or the wicked? No, of course not. But it does mean that they are challenged to learn to trust Him and not their own devices, and it also means that they learn what it means to ask Him for "our 'daily' bread."

Trusting Him also means being satisfied with what He chooses to give. This I think is the hardest thing for most people. God gives us what we need in the moment we need it. He generally doesn't give something today that we think we might need tomorrow, or six months down the line. We like to feel secure by the amount of money or possessions we can see and hold, or be told are there for us in a bank account. But all of these things can disappear in minutes, especially in this day and age when everything is electronic, and the value of hard commodities like gold, silver, and oil fluctuates from day to day.

Often what God chooses to give is not what we think we need, even if it is what we really do need at the time. God has more than our physical needs in mind. Poverty is much healthier spiritually than physical wealth because it forces us to rely on Him more and detach from trusting our own possessions and means.

I've spent years learning what living by faith means the hard way, what it is and what it isn't. Ultimately, it means trusting Him just as much for our physical life and health as we trust Him for our spiritual life and health. Maybe this is why so many people have such trouble with it, and why it is so hard to learn, because so many people who say they trust in Him spiritually don't. It's a lot harder to put your money where your mouth is when it concerns things you can see and touch.

6 | A Ramble About Ownership

If you really think about it, human ownership is a ridiculous concept. Nothing we call ours can truly ever belong to us or even originate from us. Neither our thoughts, nor our ideas, nor our bodies, nor the myriad of toys, trinkets, houses, cars, clothes, or anything else you could think of can ever truly be called "ours."

For example, who can truly own a piece of land? The land was there long before me, and it will be there long after. It neither knows, nor cares to know, that I hold a piece of paper that says I own it. And it will be rid of me in what is for it a relatively tiny amount of time.

The clothing I have in my closet. Someone else made it. Chances are that someone else wore it before me. When I die, it will not come with me, and few will uphold my rights to it after that point.

The thoughts that I think someone else thought before me. The ideas which rattle around in my mind originated with someone or something else and recombined within my own mind. I can no more lay claim to them than I can lay claim to having written "Romeo and Juliet" (of course, really William Shakespeare couldn't lay claim to that idea either as it in turn was based on an older work, as has been demonstrated). So those ideas flow from others, and as I talk about them and relay them they flow to others also. Do I then become upset because someone else has "stolen" "my" ideas?

The truth is that the idea of ownership is really just another means of us trying to make ourselves feel more secure. Or, to put it another way, the concept of ownership arises from our inherent insecurity. We are afraid of our needs not being met, and so we gather things around ourselves selfishly and tell others, "No, you can't make use of these, they're mine!" I'm afraid that if I allow someone else use of them, then I will no longer be able to use them.

This inherent insecurity of course arises from our inability to experience God from birth, which I have previously discussed. It is a concession of mercy that God does not contest it. In fact, the only person who can truly claim to "own" anything is God Himself. He created it, and He is in constant contact with it. He moves it, shapes it, and dissolves it at will.

Consider that if you were in constant experience of God as He is, ownership would be a non-issue because the issue of your own security would be a non-issue. These would be non-issues because you would experientially know His love for you, and doubt would be absurd. And this love presupposes that He too cares about your needs and would move to fulfill them. But because of our spiritual autism we cannot see it, we are blind to it.

The Scripture says, "Perfect love casts out all fear." This verse continuously goes through my mind lately. Just consider that He is perfect love, and that fear is insecurity, and that the genuine experience of Him removes all insecurity. All other concerns are thrown aside as you bask in His love for you and through you to all others. And then you come to realize that you don't need to "own" or claim "ownership" of anything at all because of His love for you.

In the end, my point is entirely proven by human death, as everything you claimed ownership over is left for someone else to clean up or make use of, even your physical remains. You no longer have control over any of it. So in the end, all of your efforts to retain control over things, ideas, and people are utterly defeated and you still lose everything. All of your efforts to acquire and hold wealth are wasted and pointless.

For this reason, the only effort with any meaning in this life is to acquire and hold the experience of God, and union with Him through Jesus Christ. To know Him through mutual love as He loves you, and you respond with love in return as His love begins to flow through you and back to Himself, radiating to others also. Cultivating and developing this love, powered by His Grace, is the only worthwhile effort because it is the only effort which is not only sustainable but will continue with you after you lose your physical remains. This is truly the only real security in life.

7 | A Ramble about Little Children

I was out playing ball with my son today. I know I don't do this enough. I've never been much of a football (or any other kind of sports) father. But, I gave my word to him that we would go out just the two of us for a little while this morning. It was good. We kicked the ball around the soccer field for a little while, and then we tried to shoot baskets (emphasis on "tried", neither of us made it), and then we wandered around the school playground by ourselves talking and finding things to do. He was excited to show me how he could make it all the way across the monkey bars, and was proud of himself when he did it on both sets of monkey bars.

As a grown up, I've been preoccupied lately with all sorts of grown up things. I've been preoccupied with where my family and I have been, and where we're going. I've been preoccupied with my own fears and my own hopes. I haven't really been present much, even if I'm in the room, and when someone tries to pull me back into the present reality I get frustrated and even angry.

My six year old son, however, has no such hang-ups. Whatever he does at this stage in his life, he's always in the moment. He gets frustrated when I try to pull him out of it into something that's hypothetical or could happen (those man to man talks which Dads try to give). He wants to show me what he can do. He wants to explore. He wants to enjoy each and every moment he has with me.

All of my kids were like this at one point in time, although the older my girls get the more preoccupied they get with other things. But when they were much younger, they couldn't care less about what *had* happened or what *would* happen, only about what *was* happening.

Jesus said, "Repent, for the Kingdom of Heaven is at hand [i.e., right here, right now]" (brackets mine). He also said that, "Unless you repent and become as little children, you can by no means enter the kingdom of heaven." There are as many commentaries as grains of sand on the beach on what these verses mean.

Here's what I think. The Kingdom of Heaven is also the Eternal Life talked about in John, and it's the intimate experience of union with God in our lives in the here and now. That experience of God, regardless of who we are, will not happen until we let go of everything that ties us down. Most especially, it won't happen until we let go of what has happened in the past, and let go of what will or might happen in the future.

Small kids have no problem with this. They, for some reason, can see that the past is gone, and the future hasn't happened yet. If it's not right now, then it doesn't exist. It's only grown-ups that have this distorted view of reality, thinking that the past and future are more important that what's right in front of us right now. Animals seem to have the same ability to be in the present at all times. Small kids tend to assume that their parents will take care of them, and that they will take care of the future; also somehow fixing whatever trouble they got into in the past. As a result, they believe they have no concerns and can focus on what matters most to them, right here, right now. It's only grown-ups that want to somehow disabuse them of that notion and get them ready for "adulthood." In so doing, we try and destroy that simple faith which they possess, and it becomes ridiculously difficult to recover once it's destroyed.

Instead of trying to encourage little kids to "grow up," Jesus told grown-ups to become like little kids. Instead of telling them to make sure they were well taken care of for the future and get their retirement plans in order, he told them not to store up money and wealth. He told them to ask God for the things they needed from day to day. In other words, He told them to live from God's paycheck to paycheck, here in the moment. He told them to do all those things which children do by nature, at which economists the world over are horrified.

Truth is, when we're afraid of what might happen, we're jumping at shadows and things which seem very real, but in fact don't even exist at the moment. If we're living in the past, we live in either a nightmare world or a fantasy world that no longer exists, and is shaped by our regrets and fears or our rosy memories. All fear is concentrated in either what has happened or what might happen, not what is happening right here and right now.

This is where we meet and experience God, right here and right now. This is where we enter the Kingdom of Heaven, right here and right now. This is where we inherit the Eternal Life, right here and right now. Sometimes we can learn a lot more from little kids than they could ever learn from us.

8 | A Ramble About Jobs or Not Having One

There is a pervasive, destructive myth among American Christians. It's Americans in general, but when it comes among Christians it takes on a whole new meaning. That myth is that you and you alone are responsible for providing for yourself and your family, and if you don't have a paying job then you're "less than" and lazy or irresponsible.

This myth is especially destructive with today's economy being what it is. I have friends with sterling resumes who used to be able to snap their fingers twice and have a high paying job lined up in a day (not as much hyperbole as you might think, by the way). These same friends have now been out of work for months on end, some up to a year or more. One good friend of mine who used to make nearly a hundred thousand a year is now unable to pay his bills, heavily in debt, and a few months from losing his house. He's put in resumes and applications, he's done the leg work. He's a crack salesman who could sell ice to an Eskimo. But in spite of all of his talent and effort, he's broke and struggling to survive with his family.

I've struggled for most of my adult life with finding and keeping work. I think the longest job I've had lasted for a few years, and those jobs I have had are nearly always on the low end of the pay scale. I have two associate's degrees and a bachelor's degree. I've spent more than five years in college, and not because I was a poor student. But there has always been this perfect storm of circumstances every so often that knocks me back down, or keeps me from progressing. It's never been because I don't want to work.

I've learned several things from trying to keep my family together and raise my kids through these storms that I hope will help those who are like my friend, whom I pray for provision and blessing every day.

The first thing I've learned is that the myth I talked about is just that, a myth. Let me ask you this. Who sends the rain and the sun for the plants to grow? Who allows them to grow and produce seed for the birds? It is God who does all this and more. A farmer or gardener can work all he wants in the hot sun, day in and day out, and his seed won't sprout or grow unless God wills it to, unless God sends the right amount of rain, and unless God allows the right amount of sun. The droughts in the southern U.S. this year, and around the world the last couple of years, should have been evidence of that. It is God who allows the bugs to come and eat your plants, or sends their predators to keep them away.

It is the same way with us. It is God who provides for us. Yes, He often uses jobs and employment as a means to do so; but ultimately it all comes from Him. You lost your job. Does this mean that He is no longer in control? Does this mean that He no longer loves you? Does this mean that somehow He doesn't care? If any of these things were possible than He would not be God. Losing our visible means of support is terrifying until we come to grips with the simple facts that God loves us and He won't abandon us.

There are times when He causes us to lose that visible means of support intentionally. It's not punishment, but it is discipline intended to force us to acknowledge that it isn't the work of our hands that puts money in the bank and food on the table. It also forces us to start stripping away all the things that we become attached to instead of Him. We start using our possessions, our employment, and the relationships around us for our security blanket instead of

Him, and this simply can't continue if we intend to pursue the path of Jesus Christ. So He removes them because He loves us. Just as any good parent would flush drugs they find down the toilet, He removes the dangerous things from us. He's more concerned about the health of our union with Him than He is about our financial health. If we look to Him, He will provide regardless of our financial state. Probably not in the way we would like, but what good parent ever gives his child every toy his child begs for?

Second, all too often Christians are beaten over the head with, "If he doesn't work, he doesn't eat." This is from 2nd Thessalonians 3. It was dealing with a situation at the church in Thessalonica where people were just living off of the dispersals at church and not contributing anything, spending their days getting into everyone else's business or doing the functional equivalent of playing video games all day and gossiping. St. Paul's concern wasn't about how much money the person was bringing in, but about whether or not he was being productive and able to contribute to others, since the path of Jesus Christ is about loving the other person and letting go of your self and your own things.

Volunteering at church or a non-profit, picking up the slack at home to help out your wife and kids, helping your neighbor out with work he or she may need done, spending time in prayer with God; these are all constructive, productive uses of time and contribute in a way which is consistent with the teaching of the Church and of Holy Scripture. In fact, these are more productive "spiritually" than trying desperately to make a bigger paycheck. The point isn't necessarily what you do as much as why and how you're doing it.

"But I need to support my family (and you do too)!" If God has prevented you (or me) from being employed in the traditional fashion then it's pointless to fight it for the moment. It's time to take a step back, take a breath, clear your mind, and focus on Him. You're not going to get another paying job unless He decides it's time for you to do so. Until that point in time, do what you can when you can, and instead of wasting all of your energy on panicking about where your next job will come from, spend it wisely on focusing on Him, trusting Him and recognizing that He is the one who provides for you. Yes, you have to swallow your pride and ask Him for help. This is fundamentally important. You can't just do this in secret. You have to be honest with Him, yourself, and others about this.

Third, how much is too much and what are your real priorities in life? Generally, people who seek to acquire large amounts of possessions and money do so because they're insecure about whether or not they'll ever have enough to be comfortable. They use it to shield themselves from facing the reality of life. If you have made the commitment to follow Jesus Christ, you can no longer do this. Wealth in general is dangerous spiritually. Poverty is a better financial state to be in for spiritual growth because it forces you back to reliance on God for your needs, and the less you possess, the less you have to be addicted or attached to, which can and will interfere with your relationship with God. There is a reason why Jesus told the rich young ruler to give up everything he had in order to achieve eternal life, and why it was common in the Apostolic Church for its members to sell everything they had and give the money to the Church for everyone to use.

Think about this very carefully. The Scripture is clear; friendship with the world is enmity with God. Jesus was pretty clear what He thought of the person who stored up possessions for his own retirement. If you choose to truly follow Him, you cannot climb the corporate ladder. There really is no middle ground, as much as many would like to pretend there is.

In the end, for those who follow Him and place knowing Him as a priority above all others, it makes little difference whether you have a paying job or not. Every circumstance you are placed in is treated the same way: it is God who provides, not you. Your focus in life should be to love others, not secure your financial future. He loves you dearly. He loves your family dearly. If you wouldn't let your kids go hungry, why do you think He would?

Part III | Practical Discipleship

1 | Of Illusions and Realities

I just went for a walk today. I live near Disneyland and the Anaheim Resort. The walk from my apartment following the major streets constitutes probably at least a square mile. My neighborhood is separated from the resort area by the I-5 freeway that divides the two halves of the square down the diagonal.

In order to reach the resort area from my neighborhood you have to walk all the way around the freeway. There are no paths or shortcuts across or under it. The freeway exits for the resort area lead straight into it, with "no right turn" and "no left turn" signs posted right as the exit meets Anaheim Boulevard. What's odd about this is that the exit terminates at a traffic light, and a right or left turn would be no more dangerous there than at any other traffic light. The entrances to the freeway from the resort are also just as singular in purpose. They lead straight out of the resort and do not permit any side trips into the surrounding city and neighborhoods.

As you walk along Harbor Boulevard next to the Disneyland resort's main vehicle entrance you are surrounded by immaculate hotels suited to nearly every budget, restaurants and eateries ranging from McDonald's to Denny's, the Jolly Roger to Bubba Gump Shrimp Co. All of these places are staffed by very friendly, even perky, young adults and teenagers. There are people who are obvious tourists everywhere. The atmosphere is friendly, inviting, upbeat, and in constant motion. All of it is watched over by both armed and unarmed security who stay mostly out of sight and work tirelessly to blend in with the rest of the background until a problem arises which calls for their intervention. And there are also the Anaheim police officers making regular patrols on foot, bicycle, and patrol car through the parks and resorts.

As I walked through it all and somewhat blended in, several thoughts occurred to me. Most of the people who come here will only come once in their lives. They will have saved up thousands of dollars to come here, spend a few nights in a hotel, and escape into the carefully orchestrated and sanitized world which this half of the square mile presents away from their "real" world wherever "back home" may be. They don't want to remember their bills, their employers, their schools, or their real lives. They want to leave them, if only for a few days out of their entire lives, and be able to forget that they exist by immersing themselves in the family friendly illusions and dreams that the Resort Area offers.

On the other side of the freeway is my neighborhood. We live there because the rent is inexpensive . . . for Orange County at least. It is a predominantly Spanish speaking neighborhood. On one major street corner there is a supermarket in which it is almost a requirement to know a little Spanish to purchase anything. The produce is fresh, ripe, and cheap. There's a real butcher, a real bakery, and a small "Deli" of sorts that sells tacos, burritos, rotisserie chicken, menudo, chorizo, and other dishes of which it would be redundant to say they are authentically Mexican. I don't think those preparing them would know how to prepare anything else, and you're on your own if you can't say at least part of your order in Spanish. Nearby is a book and music store which proudly proclaims "Musica, Libros, Peliculas" with no English translations anywhere on the signage. There are a few fast food places as well.

My apartment complex is one of several along my street in various stages of disrepair. As you walk down the street on a Saturday, it is common to see people holding yard sales and trading their old things for someone else's old things. I'm not sure if any of it actually ever leaves this neighborhood after being sold. Young Hispanic mothers play with their babies and watch their young children play. Older kids chase each other around. Boys strike up impromptu games of soccer in their yards, or in the school playground that is behind my complex. At night, they play street hockey in the school's parking lot.

As I come home from work late at night, I often find several of the men who live next to and near us surrounding an old barely working television in the mailbox area. They are generally watching a soccer game or a boxing game and being just as raucous and celebratory about it as if they were actually there. Other times they just stand or sit with each other, drinking a few beers, swapping stories, insults, dreams, hopes, or fears. One of my neighbors washes cars and fixes bicycles out of his garage. As far as I can tell, they work when they can get work, and share in each other's lives when they can't.

There are police who watch this area as well. They watch it like hawks, waiting for the kill. I see them patrol it several times a day, and supposedly with good reason. I have on more than one occasion caught the distinctive odor of marijuana wafting through my windows, or around the stairwell. I have seen strangers simply sitting on the bench out front as if they were waiting for someone. A few times, strangers have come to my door with the shakes looking to acquire what I think was cocaine, judging by the colorful names that they were giving what they wanted. I have also often come home to find police units parked in the middle of the street. The officers were out with guns drawn on teenagers lying on the ground with hands on their heads. The man whose daughter we were babysitting for a time stopped coming when an undercover officer drew his gun on him as he was getting out of his car. His pregnant girlfriend who was in the car lost their child from the shock.

Illusions and realities. As human beings we fight, scrimp, strive, and spend everything we have saved to achieve the illusion and hold on to it, even if only for a few brief moments of our lives. We guard that illusion and even that hope of illusion jealously, and like the security in the background, when it becomes in danger of being invaded by reality, we strike back with ferocity to force reality back into submission. But in the end, the illusion must fade when the money runs out. That's what illusions do. And when the money or resources run out, it doesn't just fade, it throws you out as though an unwelcome vagrant, without kindness, without pity, without remorse, and without compassion; all in the name of maintaining it's image. And we are left again with the shock of reality as it is, made all the more painful because of the lost sweetness that we have so freshly tasted.

Reality isn't sweet. It isn't well manicured. It's life lived in the here and now with all that goes with it. Reality demands that you look at the present, and doesn't have time for illusion. Reality lives, loves, laughs, cries, shouts, gets angry, bleeds, and dies, sometimes all in the same instant. It demands your full attention and makes you pay for it. It sets the consequences of your actions in front of you and demands that you deal with them in the here and now, and will not be put off until tomorrow. Reality is the hardworking older man who lives by washing cars out of his garage. Reality is the group of kids who can't afford any more than just enjoying being with each other and playing soccer together. Reality is a boxing match shared on an old TV with gusto and joy, or a game of pool played on a table rescued from a dumpster. Reality is the kid who can't find love or acceptance at home and so joins with others like himself to compose a new code of friendship, honor, and loyalty, even if it means doing so at the expense of other's peace and security. Reality is the young mother who hides her bruises as well as she can, and hopes her husband doesn't come home drunk again.

We don't encounter God in the illusion. God is. He exists. He is right here, right now. He laughs, cries, shouts, weeps, shares, bleeds, hopes, loves, and dies right along with us here in reality. He feels it when the young mother has to take another backhand from her husband. He weeps with the older grandmother who doesn't know how to help her grandson find his way out of his dark path. He empathizes when the young man can't find work, and knows just how he feels. We encounter God in the reality, where we don't want to be.

And when all is said and done, the illusion will finally fade and end. The buzz of whatever kind will pass away. The money will run out, the lights will fade, the party will be over. And then all that is left is Reality, where He is. Where He always and eternally Is. Where we don't want to be and have been fighting desperately to stay away from, and to stay away from Him.

There is no true joy without sorrow. No true pleasure without pain. No true sanity, without losing one's mind in order to find it. As Christians, living in the "resurrection life" is often spoken of. But in order for one to be resurrected, they must first die. That which has not died cannot by nature be resurrected. And so the resurrection that is commonly proclaimed is often only an illusion, and, more often than not, one which is easy to see past given enough time. Truth will always make itself known as truth. Those who most often preach this kind of resurrected life do so for fear of the Cross, and the Reality it requires us to embrace. The one we don't want to embrace.

Illusions and realities. Jesus Christ spent long hours and days giving everything he had to the sick, the demonized, the lame, the crippled, the blind, the deaf, the dumb, and the dead. He spent most of His time in neighborhoods like mine with people who today could be drug dealers, young abused mothers, young men with no hope, old men with shattered dreams, societal outcasts, revolutionaries, and radicals. He set out to heal and bring healing to them all, body, mind, and spirit. Several of them were His closest friends and students, and were responsible for carrying His message and salvation to the ends of the earth. If he shunned and criticized and policed anyone, it was those who fought to maintain their own illusions of power, security, and authority . . . and who did so no matter what it may cost anyone who got in their way, including Jesus Christ Himself. Jesus would likely be hanging out mostly in my neighborhood, not at the resort.

Are we going to follow Him or not?

2 | Rambling about Faith

"There is no spoon."

I watched the Matrix the other day. I don't know why, it had been a while since I'd seen it, but I just had this urge to watch it. I remember my philosophy professor telling us in class one time how ecstatic all philosophy professors were that this movie had been made. It's always been one of my favorites.

As I was watching, I got to the scene with the kid in the Oracle's apartment who was bending spoons with his mind. When Neo asked him how he did it, he said to try and remember the truth, that there is no spoon.

This phrase, this concept, keeps repeating itself in my mind. "There is no spoon." Of course what he meant was that in reality, the spoon itself was only a construct of the Matrix's program. He said, "Do not try and bend the spoon. That's impossible. Instead, only try to realize the truth . . . There is no spoon . . . Then you'll see that it is not the spoon that bends; it is only yourself." (A "Potential Kid", *The Matrix*.)

Jesus said that if we had faith the size of a mustard seed, which is ridiculously small, we could tell a mountain to uproot itself and replant itself in the sea, and it would obey. Of course, attempting to uproot a mountain just by telling it to is impossible. I'm sure many have tried faithfully.

But let's look deeply at that mountain for a minute. It's largely made out of rock and stone. This rock and stone is made up of various elements that have combined chemically to form granite, basalt, sandstone, etc. Those elements in turn are made up of certain combinations of protons, neutrons, and electrons. These sub-atomic particles are themselves, in the case of protons and neutrons, made up of quarks. Quarks and electrons have been revealed to be energy vibrations of a certain frequency and spin. That energy is of course derived from the only Source of all energy who used the energy of His own Existence, all that truly Exists as such, as the building blocks of all created existence.

Like all else created, the mountain relies on God for its very existence, for its very foundation. It, in reality, is no different than we are. It is only our perception of the mountain which we derive from our senses and experiences which makes it so much bigger, so much stronger, so much more solid and massive than we are.

When God asks us to trust Him, when he asks us to do something by faith, what He's asking us to remember is that there is no spoon. He is not bound by our senses or perceptions. Should He choose it, the mountain can cease to exist instantaneously, as all He needs to do is cause those certain energy vibrations that form the mountain to cease vibrating. As it is all the energy of His own Existence at play, ultimately, it is as simple for Him to do this as it is for me to breathe in or out, or to flex the muscles of my finger.

If this is true, then why doesn't He always move those mountains when we tell them to move? I believe first that it is because we don't ask Him, we tell Him. Never a wise idea. At best it causes a good round of laughter. At worst . . .

Second, do we have, and keep, that relationship with Him to where He would? All relationships take work to maintain. All friendships must be renewed periodically, and all marriages must involve a great deal of emotional, psychological, and physical intimacy to stay healthy. This takes action on the part of both parties. Both parties must spend quality time with one another. An old friend might accede to a request based on your past relationship with them even if you haven't seen them for ten years, but if you've repeatedly blown them off for ten years after they've tried to get together with you, how likely are they to be agreeable to it?

Third, think about Him as your Father. My kids ask me for stuff all the time. When we're at Wal-Mart they ask for toys, or drinks, or candy, or shoes, etc. There are times when I accede to these things because I know they enjoy them and I enjoy watching them enjoy them. There are more times when I don't because I know that if I do, they will get more spoiled and cease to appreciate what they have. When they ask for lunch, or dinner, or just basic every day provision, do I withhold it to make them appreciate it more? No, of course not. They need to eat. They need clothes to wear. They need certain daily provisions, and it's my job as Daddy to see to it that they get them. Then there are times when they ask for something in their own childlike way not understanding all the implications of what they're asking. Then, a lot of times, I know that they don't have the knowledge base for me to explain all of my reasons for saying no. And I just have to ask them to trust me on it.

There have been plenty of times like this last example where I've prayed for something that seemed perfectly reasonable to me at the time, and would seem to be what He would pray for, and then He doesn't do it. But as the time passes by He has me reason through some of the ramifications of what I was asking. It's not that the request is necessarily bad, it's just that it isn't the best thing for everyone involved. And sometimes, it really isn't the right time for it.

But when he asks us to trust Him, He's asking us to remember that there is no spoon. When He asks us to walk up to the mountain and tell it to move out of the way, He's asking us to remember that there is no mountain irregardless of what our senses are telling us. There is only Him.

He tells us to get out of the boat and walk on the water. We respond back and say, "What about the hurricane and the fact that water can't support my weight?" His response, "What water? All there truly is, is Me." He tells us to feed five thousand with five loaves of bread and a couple of trout. Are we feeding them with bread and fish? Or are we feeding them with Him?

He is the One who does not move through space and time, but space and time move through Him. He is the One who does not exist in creation, but all creation Exists in Him.

It is our perceptions that must change, not the world around us. Do we perceive rock and stone and sea and sky, or do we perceive being surrounded by Him? In the Matrix, all most anyone can see is what their minds are telling them is real. Such as Cypher, who in the end didn't care that the steak wasn't real, as long as his mind told him it tasted good. But then there was Neo, who in the end didn't see the walls, the floors, the people, or the buildings. All he could see was the Matrix code underlying everything, and through this change in his perception his experience was changed, and thus his world was changed completely.

God asks us, by faith, to not see the rock and stone and storms and sea. He asks us to see the Code, Himself, which underlies it all, and with this change in our perception of the world, to go forward trusting Him.

Is there a mountain in your life He's asking you to trust Him to move? Is there a sea He's asking you to walk through on dry ground? Is there a raging storm in which He's asking you to get out of the boat and walk on the water? Remember . . . there is no spoon.

3 | A Ramble about Personal Demons

I recently went through a process of healing from my own personal demons. Some of them were figurative, and some of them perhaps literal depending on how you look at it. These demons have haunted me for years. They were demons of rejection, demons of autism, demons of needing attention, demons of striving to prove myself and defend myself to anyone and everyone else, and demons of failure.

I am learning in the afterglow of this healing, however, that these demons do not give up, ever. If they are literal, then they have been around for millennia, and are easily capable of outlasting me and wearing me down. They don't seem to ever get tired and just give up. They hammer and hammer and hammer away. Sometimes they let up, and then when I least expect it they attack again.

It has only been within the last few days that I realized freedom from such demons has nothing to do with a once and for all triumph where they go sulking away in defeat, never to return. That would be great. But instead, it has to do with how I respond, or don't respond, to their attacks from this point onward.

These demons don't attack my strong points. Like any competent tactician they attack my weakest points, those in which I have already been hurt or compromised in some way. They whisper little lies into my ears knowing that somewhere within me a part of me might be willing to believe them. They work tirelessly to get me to agree with them, and then once they have that staging point, they continue their assault further in.

One of my favorite movies is *Little Buddha*. In this movie there is a scene which depicts the temptations of the Buddha by Mara (similar to the temptations of Christ in the desert by the Devil). The one image which stands out to me in this scene is where Mara assaults the Buddha with hundreds if not thousands of archers, and they all shoot flaming arrows at the Buddha as he sits serenely under a tree. As the arrows fall, they become flowers and blossoms, falling harmlessly around him.

Being delivered from my personal demons, I realized, doesn't mean they never attack me again. It means their attacks are never able to harm me again. It means that there are no more places for me to agree with them in, there are no more weak or compromised areas for them to assault. So like the scene above they can shoot all the flaming arrows they want but they will only fall harmlessly like soft flower petals, much to the archers' frustration.

Most of their temptations have to do with trying to get me to react according to my experience, biology, or past history. For example, if I have a past history of being or feeling rejected by people, then they want to use that rejection to influence my present situation and get me to respond according to that rejection. This then can translate into anger or bitterness against those people who rejected me in the past and I can spend my time dwelling there in my mind. It can also translate into mistrust for people's motives in the present and absolute despair for the future, or a constant striving so that somehow things will be better in the future. It can also become an attitude of "I'll show them."

It doesn't help to deny that I have this weakness concerning my past either; in fact it makes it that much worse as I try to deal with these attacks on my own. Denying that I have a problem only provides another compromised area for them to renew their assault, and then I'm fighting unsuccessfully on two different fronts.

It really gets bad when I try to deal with these things on my own without the prayer, support, and intercession of friends and family. Whether I recognize that I am weak or compromised or not, I need their help and support. It is like a favorite story of mine from Star Trek. It goes like this: A great windstorm was approaching the walls of a city. They rang the storm bell and hurried everyone into the safety of the walls. All went in except one, a warrior who was renowned for his courage in battle. The ruler of the city tried to convince him to take refuge in the city, but he would not. He said that he would stand outside the walls and make the wind respect him. The ruler gave up, honored his request, and went inside. The next morning after the storm had passed they found that warrior's body smashed against the city gates. The moral of the story is "The wind doesn't respect a fool" (paraphrased from "Rightful Heir", *Star Trek: The Next Generation*). All too often, whether it is conscious or not, I declare that I'm going to stand and make the hurricane of these attacks respect me. My own pride and arrogance leads me to believe that I can handle these attacks on my own without humbling myself and seeking the shelter of prayer from friends and family.

Our personal demons attack and prey on our fears, our hopes, and our attachments. We become attached to our anger, our bitterness, or our mistrust. They seem like familiar tools and friends who have gotten us through tough times before, but in truth they were the kind of friends who would show you a good time and then leave you battered and bleeding in an alley. We become attached to our possessions, our loved ones, and our self image, all the while trying desperately to maintain the lie that we will never lose them, when in fact we will eventually have to lose all of them. This is the nature of mortality, temporality, and impermanence. We become attached to our lives, fighting valiantly to stave off death for as long as possible, all the while refusing to see the truth that death is the *only* way to resurrection.

Death is in fact what our personal demons fear most. They fear us dying to our self-image, dying to our possessions, dying to our anger and bitterness, and dying to our refusal to accept change. They especially fear the death of the Cross. They fear what it means. They can't attack a corpse and expect it to respond favorably to them. It is this death which turns flaming arrows into flower blossoms, and it is a belief and trust in and experience of God's love and care for us, at least for me, that fuels that death. It is our faith in and acceptance of our death with Christ on His Cross that shields us from these attacks and renders them harmless. And it is precisely the experience of this death that allows us to experience Him; allows us to enter the Kingdom of Heaven and possess His Eternal Life here and now. It is like taking the "red pill" (see *Matrix*) and finally being able to see the world as it truly is.

The attacks will persist. I've accepted that now. But how effective they are depends largely on my continuous acceptance of my death with Him, and His love and acceptance of me. They know this. They fear it, and over the last few days I feel like their attacks have been stepped up. They have blind-sided me a few times now right in those places where I first professed healing. By the Grace of God He saw me through it, not allowing me to be blinded again. I am learning through these stepped-up attacks that the best place for me during these attacks is the refuge of being in Him and in the prayers and intercessions of family and friends, in the Body or with Christ. I should not risk fighting them on my own, as this is what they want. It's a tough lesson to learn, but in the end it is they who will be frustrated, upset, and alone as they realize they are beating on a dead corpse.

4 | Another Ramble about Demons

If someone insulted you, threatened you, hit you, and tried to hurt you, would you be angry with them and hold it against them? What if someone was egging them on? What if they were being provoked by someone else, quietly, to do something they might like to do but would otherwise restrain themselves from doing? What if they were mentally unbalanced, and you had a decent relationship with them on their good days? Would you still hold it against them?

I can't say I don't believe in demons, either from a doctrinal perspective or from an experiential one. In theology, we talk about fallen spiritual beings that are themselves, for all intents and purposes, psychotic and insane by definition. They continue to make harmful choices for themselves and pursue harmful courses of action towards others, even after experiencing that such choices will only result in more harm to themselves and a continuation of their downward spiral.

In my experiences, I see the fruit of the activity of demons all the time, and experience their attacks on my own heart and mind. I watch, feeling powerless (whether I am or not), as people I care about relive past trauma, have their worst fears pounded through their minds, are physically assaulted, and more. I have, more often than I want to, seen this activity in the eyes of certain individuals. It is something about the way the eyes look.

One of the more revealing aspects of the writings of the *Philokalia* is that the authors constantly refer to these same demons. They make no pretenses as to what they believe to be the sources of the quietly provoking thoughts, images, and fantasies that run through their minds. Such provocations often begin with something relatively benign. Perhaps they begin with a thought, a desire for something simple, or even a desire to do something good, but then it turns very quickly into a downward spiral that one must fight to get out of.

There are also figurative demons. These are not literal fallen spirits, but often the effect is no different. These are past traumas, past memories, past beliefs, past hopes, and past fears. These are a product of the person's own mind and they can do almost as much damage as the psychotic spirit. All too often, they probably work in conjunction, making the spirit's machinations that much easier.

The person isn't possessed, but they do assent to the behavior suggested to them quietly, believing that it is something they really want to do. This is heartbreaking to see when it happens. The person doesn't even realize what's going on. They are oblivious to it, and if you should address the evil behind it, they will believe you are attacking them and not trying to help them. This is all a part of the twisted game. Demons don't have to take full possession of a person to bend them to do what they want. They can do it more easily by suggestion, by playing on their fears, their aspirations, and their appetites. The Fathers of the *Philokalia* continuously address three "passions" to constantly guard against: the desire for sensual pleasure, the desire to possess things, and the desire for self-esteem. These three things are referred to as the three main gates which demons use to bend us to do what they want, and the fathers wrote extensively about guarding against them through poverty, humility, and self-control.

It is popular in charismatic and evangelical movements to "cast out demons." I can't really comment on the effectiveness of their techniques or tactics. Exorcism is a well established rite within the

Church and every division of it, but it generally only focuses on full blown possession, and that state seems to be the only one which traditional exorcism is equipped to deal with. How do you exorcise a person who is not possessed, but who assents to demonic suggestion? What do you do when they still have full control over their free will and choices, and they choose the demonic action not knowing from where the suggestion came?

Can you really be angry with the person who is a victim of both their own choices as well as something else egging them on? What if it was you? As much as I might try to guard myself from such suggestions, I know for a fact that I get little whispers all the time. They play on my fears, yes; but even more often they play on my ego, introducing little fantasies about how great I am or how great I could be. One of the more effective inroads with me is through personal comforts: wanting to watch certain programs or read certain books that are benign enough in and of themselves, but distract me long enough for them to take it further. I get angry with myself for my own weakness, but it doesn't change the fact that I'm weak.

Can you really be angry with the person who is weak, seeing that you share the same weakness that gets used against you? Can you be angry with the person who hits you when it could just as well have been you hitting someone else on a different day? Can you really pass judgment on someone who acts on his or her fears when you do it as well?

I see the activity of demons all the time. I see it in people's eyes, in their actions, and in what they say. I also see these same people going about completely oblivious to that activity in their own lives, ignorant, and even though complicit, nearly innocent. Can I really be angry with them?

5 | A Ramble about Fasting

I hate fasting.

I've never seen the usefulness of it. I remember a guy I knew a long time ago once telling me that he had tried to fast, only to be reminded by his stomach that it was time to eat. It got to the point, as he described it, that his hunger drowned out any spiritual thoughts or motives to the point where he just gave up and ate something so that he could clear his mind.

My experiences with fasting have generally been similar. I've tried fasting before. I actually went a whole week without eating anything. I wanted it to be for spiritual reasons, but in reality it was more to see whether or not I could do it. I did, and then promptly got diarrhea with the first meal I had after the week was up. In spite of my protestations to the contrary, the reality was that the only benefit it brought me was a bit of weight loss, hardly spiritual in nature.

In many ways, I've been on forced fasts this past week. I've been eating less than I usually do, by necessity. I've been getting less sleep than I probably need. I've not had any real alone time for four days, and there are other little assaults on my physical comfort as well that just . . . prick, a little here, and a little there. In short, I've been miserable. And the cherry on top of this cake is that I seem to be coming down with the flu as well (never mind the asthma and chest congestion I'm still fighting from months ago).

Yesterday or the day before the conversation between God and Satan came to my mind from the book of Job. In it, Satan has pretty much ruined Job's life and destroyed everything he loves and holds dear, and Job's still praising God. So, Satan says this, "Skin for skin! A man will give up everything he has to save his life. But reach out and take away his health, and he will surely curse you to your face!" Truth is, while I don't recall Job ever cursing God to His face, he did get a lot more whiny after that in asking for explanations.

We don't like to admit it, or at least I don't, but Satan's analysis of the human response was, in most cases, spot on. No one ever accused Satan of being an idiot or unobservant. Psychotic perhaps, but definitely not an idiot. We seem to be willing to part with quite a bit, but when it touches our physical comfort, that's when things really get personal.

I think that's the biggest lesson for me in all of this. Does my physical comfort and well being dictate the terms of my relationship with God? I've written before about having to die in order to be resurrected, but ironically, the body always seems to be the last thing in which I--and probably not just me--am willing to commit to the cross. I always use the excuse of needing a clear head, and not wanting to be distracted from communion with the Lord by being hungry, or having some unfulfilled physical need or urge. It makes sense to me in the moment.

The truth is that all too often I am ruled, not by the Spirit, but by my stomach. Like the proverbial "momma", when it ain't happy, ain't nobody happy. And this is also the place where it seems unclean things like to attack the hardest, because they know it's a sure-fire weak point.

The truth is that you can't serve two masters, and often we try. The body has it's needs, and they must be cared for, but, as one Buddhist author whom I respect highly puts it, the body is like an injury or a wound. You must care for it very carefully, all the while treating it and helping it to heal. One doesn't indulge an injury or a wound in order to make it worse, but you do baby it just a little in order to help it get better. The truth is, you can't serve both God and your physical appetites. Either they become subject to the death of the cross, or they master you. There isn't any middle ground here.

I don't like this. I think it sucks, and I whine and complain just like Job when my body gets touched in any way. Thing is though, Jesus didn't, and He didn't use my excuses about needing a clear head to face temptation either. In fact, He refused to turn stones to bread when He hadn't eaten for forty days. Most people who reach that point are generally either delirious with hunger, or just plain dead. He went up against Satan himself in that state.

He didn't use those excuses when the crowds wouldn't give Him and His students any alone time either. His students asked Him, almost literally in the Greek, to blow them off and give Himself a break. He refused, and ministered to the crowds until each one of the thousands who came to Him was healed, and only then did He let them go. Today, I think He would be recommended to counseling for avoiding burnout.

And then there's the cross itself. Vicious scourgings, massive blood loss, total physical and emotional humiliation, and finally death, after having massive railroad size spikes driven through the nerves of his feet and wrists.

In many respects, Jesus fasted physically every day of His life even when He was eating and drinking. He didn't let His bodily appetites, though He had them like everyone else, control Him or what He did. I am sure there are times when His body screamed at Him and made Him dizzy enough to collapse. But His body was made subject to His cross long before He was nailed to it, like every other aspect of His life.

I don't like fasting, but then I'm sure He didn't either. I'm fairly certain the cross was no fun at all. I write a lot here about submitting to death and letting everything go, and my physical appetites and body need to be a part of that. But because it's so intrinsically tied to my "self" it becomes that much harder to let go of, especially when it's little things that keep gnawing at me. But He did it. And He asks us to pick up our crosses and follow Him. Man, this is going to hurt

. . . I'm fairly certain somewhere along the way, He said the same thing to Himself, and then kept walking towards Golgotha.

6 | A Ramble about the Storm

I 'm sitting in my bed with my laptop perched on my lap trying to remember all those things I had wanted to write a ramble about, and the truth is that I'm drawing a blank as I sit here. It's probably stress and exhaustion. We've had a pretty tough few weeks, and both my wife and I are beginning to feel the strain. We feel caught in a huge storm of actions, reactions, hopes, fears, and circumstances that seems a little like a hurricane bearing down on us right now. In the middle of all of this, the Lord has been providing for us when by all rights we should have been blown away by the forces at work.

It's really easy to look at the storm and be afraid. Hurricanes do a tremendous amount of damage, whether they're literal, spiritual, emotional, financial, or physical, or some combination of all or any of the above. The come on slowly, and all you can do is sit and wait, trying to prepare and riding them out in some kind of a safe shelter or refuge. If you've survived through the eye and come out on the other side, you then have to assess the damage and see if rebuilding is even possible. Sometimes it is, and sometimes you just have to cut your losses and move on, hard as it may be.

The storm swirling around us right now doesn't seem to want to let up in any reasonable amount of time (at least to me). The temptation is there to go to the door, open it, and just peek out at the storm to see if it's getting any lighter. The problem is, the minute you open the door and look at the storm, the storm invites itself in and tries to drag you out into it. No, the best thing is to stay put in your place of refuge until you're given the all clear.

It's easy for me to look at the circumstances swirling around us. It's easy for me to look at things I and others have done and react in anger or guilt. It's easy for me to take a possible future and blow it all out of proportion as our only lifeline. It's far, far too easy for me to try and open the door to check on the storm, and this is when I make it worse, not better.

The thing about storms is that they can actually be of great benefit to the environment. They bring rain to water the ground. What we call firestorms here in Southern California, as deadly and as fierce as they can be, also burn out all the dead brush which lays there and collects. Storms tend to come in and destroy what human beings have built up. Funny thing about what human beings often build is that these constructions often destroy the natural environment and surrounding habitats. It destroys the things we've worked so hard to build up, the things which we become attached to, the things which so often build up like dead brush and cause ruin in our own lives. Storms come in and start the process of renewal by first destroying everything in their paths.

Our refuge, our place of hope and safety is in the Lord Himself. It's not in what we have built for ourselves. It's not in some possible future, or some past event. It's right here, right now, in Him. In the scriptures, Peter walked on water during a terrible windstorm on the Sea of Galilee by keeping his eyes on Jesus the whole time. It was only when he started looking at the storm that he began to sink. Our place of refuge from the storm has to be something that the storm cannot destroy, and that place of refuge is Jesus Christ. Remaining in Him as He told us to do. When we're given the all clear everything we built may be gone, but we will still remain safe in our refuge.

7 | The Lesson of the Quarter

I t's a question I've come up against on several intelligence tests now. If you flip a quarter four times, and it comes up heads all four times, assuming that it is a normal quarter, what is the chance that it will come up tails when it is flipped the fifth time?

When I first heard this question my mind set to work trying to figure it out, and I started encountering all sorts of mathematical calculations. A friend of mine who had heard the question as well came up with the answer immediately, and I admit, I felt pretty dumb.

The answer of course is that the quarter has a 50% chance of coming up tails, just like it did every other time it was flipped. And my friend then stated the obvious; "The quarter doesn't remember how many times it's been flipped!"

The quarter has no memory. It is always in the ever present "now." It can't go back and reason out that it's high time it came up tails as opposed to heads, or be predisposed against coming up tails and try for heads. It can't do that. It can only succumb to the whims of gravity, rotation, and chance, and only God knows for certain how it will land.

In assuming that the previous flips had any bearing on the question at hand, I was doing something that only human beings do. I was bringing the past into the matter at hand when it had no business being there.

Human beings in general like to dwell in or on one of two places, either the past or the future, and we filter the present through either the way things have been or the way we would like them to be. If we would sit and look honestly at the present situation, we would realize that the past is done and gone and no present situation will present itself exactly like anything that has happened before. We would also realize that the future hasn't happened yet, and is integrally tied with the choices we make in the here and now, for better or worse. But we don't think like that.

In my own situation which I am facing now, I have realized that I am allowing everything that has happened to me in the past, either good or bad, to influence how I react to the present. It is producing within me all sorts of negative reactions because of the memories associated with it. But the truth of the matter is that the situation is different, as each moment in time is unique to itself, and the factors of the equation have changed significantly. But because it resembles the same scenario, I drag all of those memories back out and try to apply it to something on which it has no bearing.

The quarter has no memory of the past. It flips and lands with the same chance that it had every other time because it is focused in and on the present moment. One could argue that this is because the quarter has no mind to remember with. True, it doesn't. But then how often do our own minds cloud the present moment with needless reminders of the past?

Leaving the past in the past is tough. Letting the future be the future can be even tougher. We tend to pin our hopes and dreams in either one, not realizing that we live in neither. I think that we also need to realize that we don't meet or experience God in the past or the future. We experience Him in the here and now. "Repent, for the kingdom of heaven is at hand." This could be paraphrased as "The Kingdom of God is right here, right now."

The quarter doesn't spend time remembering the failures or successes of the past. It also doesn't spend time hoping that it will get a better result with future flips. It is only focused on the one flip, in the moment, right here and right now.

8 | A Ramble about Love

As a Priest, I have done a lot of pre-marital counseling. My church required it, and I always felt that I held a responsibility for each marriage I performed just as much as the couple I married. I was declaring before God and the state that these people were ready to make the commitment to become man and wife. As a result, I made it my business to prepare them however I could in the brief amount of time I was usually given before the marriage. This amount of time could range anywhere from a week to several months.

As part of the pre-marital counseling I would generally give them what I called my "schpiel" about love and relationships. I am something of an amateur Greek scholar, having studied that language for eighteen years, and so I based my schpiel on the words in Greek translated as "love." Not every Greek scholar may agree with my definitions, but for the purposes of the "schpiel" they served very well.

The word love is translated in Greek often by three primary root words: eros, philia, and agape. These represent of spectrum of ideas that we sum up in the one English word, love. Each of these kinds of love are natural expressions of stages in relationships, and each have their own proper place.

The first word, eros, sits at one end of the spectrum. This is the kind of love which is most defined by a desire to be with someone and the need or craving to have that desire fulfilled. It is highly charged with feelings and passions. The problem with eros is that you can't build a relationship on it and expect it to last. It's like trying to build a structure, not just on sand, but on the incoming waves. The reason for this is because it is so highly dependent on how we *feel* about the other person. Feelings come, and feelings go. There is nothing wrong with this; it's the nature of feelings. And when our feelings about the other person have begun to die down and the craving to be with that person has been satisfied, then if that was the only foundation for the relationship, there is nothing left. This is often why so many relationships and marriages fail so quickly, and also why many relationships are on a roller coaster ride, because eros disappears and reappears with the tides of feelings. It has always been my counsel that you can't build a marriage, or any relationship, on eros.

The next type of love is philia. This is the kind of love that grows between two people as they relate to each other over time. It is the kind of love shared between close friends, parent and child, siblings, or a married couple who have been together for many years. It is an attachment and affection for the other person that is independent of the desire to be with them, but maintains a more stable feeling of attachment. The problem with building a relationship on, or holding a relationship together with, philia is that it, too, is still based on how you feel about the other person. There is a real danger with philia as well, because over time little annoyances tend to build up between the two people, which, if left unresolved, turn into a real bitterness and resentment. The attachment to the other person remains even as the feelings turn from affection to repulsion, and what was a deep connection between the two people can invert and become a deep hatred, made all the worse by the continued bond between them. This doesn't always happen. It depends on the couple, and many try to build their relationship based on this. Some even succeed. But the truth is that you can't really build a relationship on philia either without running the risk of disappointment and devastating failure, because it, too, is based on how you feel about the other person. Philia lies in between the two ends of the spectrum.

The final type of love is agape, and this is a word that most Christians, and even many non-Christians, have heard at least somewhere even if they don't know what it means. This is the other end of the spectrum from eros. Agape isn't about how you feel about a person, and isn't about what attachment you possess to that person. Agape can be defined as the choice to care about the best interests and well-being of the other person irregardless of how that person makes you feel. It is a love that, as phrased by Thich Nhat Hanh, "looks deeply" at the other person. It takes into account who they are, where they've been, who's had input into their lives, and finally, no matter what they've done, acts in their best interests in spite of what they may have done to you or for you. It says "I am going to care about you and for you no matter what you have done." Two of the best examples of this are the stories of the Good Samaritan, where a man takes care of and tends his avowed enemy, and where in the Gospels Jesus prays for and begs the Father to forgive those same men who are at the moment brutally torturing Him and executing Him through crucifixion. At some point in every relationship, in order for that relationship to continue, either party must make the choice to care about the other person and forgive them no matter how that person has hurt them or made them feel. Because the truth is that in every relationship or marriage, one person will do something which will knowingly or unknowingly hurt the other person and thoroughly squash any good feelings, romantic or otherwise, for that person. If that relationship isn't grounded squarely in agape then it will most likely fail. The hardest part is that agape absolutely requires us to sacrifice some part of ourselves to meet its demands, just like Jesus sacrificed every part of Himself to meet its demands for us.

Every relationship takes hard work and sacrifice to maintain. Every marriage and every friendship take action and understanding on the part of both parties to continue. Most people realize this in one form or another. One relationship that we tend to forget about on this count is our relationship with God through Jesus Christ. There is a tendency among Christians of any stripe to think that God has already done all of the hard work through Jesus, and now we can just do whatever we want. It is true that Jesus Christ, literally, went to hell and back for our relationship with Him. But it is my opinion that the work of a relationship doesn't stop with one party making huge sacrifices for the other, and the other not doing anything at all.

I have often remarked that the Sacrament of Baptism is like the Sacrament of Marriage. The major difference is that in the one you are making a lifelong commitment to another human being. In Baptism, you are making an eternal commitment to Almighty God when you are conjoined to Jesus Christ. Imagine if, after your wedding day, your spouse chose never to tell you that they loved you, started seeing other people, or just totally ignored you or became indifferent to you and how you felt about what they did. How would you feel, especially if you had made great sacrifices for your marriage to even happen, if your spouse refused to put any work into it at all? I can already tell you that what would result is a broken marriage. Even if divorce didn't result, estrangement, abuse, and severe emotional pain would.

I am also learning through my own relationship with Him that our relationship with Him tends to follow the same patterns that I described above. We go through a period of a deep craving and longing to be with Him. We develop an affection for Him, and an attachment to Him. We have normal emotional responses to the One we love. But like any feelings for anyone else, these die down and subside. If we feel He has hurt us, we may not want to admit it to ourselves and blame ourselves for it. Or we may outright blame Him, and develop a bitterness and resentment that will build up. Just as we all know married couples to whom this has happened, so we also know Christians to whom this has happened. Our expectations with God often mirror our expectations in our human relationships. Our feelings and perceptions of injury are real and they feel justified to us, even if they are not justified in the absolute sense.

The word used in scripture every time Jesus gives the command to love is agape. This is true whether He says love your enemies, your neighbor, each other, or God Himself. What He's saying is to do the hard work of choosing to care about these people no matter how they make you feel or what you feel they have done to you. This includes God. This isn't about taking the moral high ground against Him, as if that were even possible; rather it's about looking deeply at who He is, knowing that what He does, He does because He loves, and because it's the best thing for everyone involved, even if it hurts. But refusing to admit that hurt helps no one, and causes harm to the relationship. It's about knowing that He sees everything and everyone, not one particle of an atom moves without Him knowing about it, not one thought escapes His attention, not one intention slips by Him. It's about trusting that agape He chooses with you, and responding with agape in return. This takes hard work and sacrifice of ourselves in order to maintain, especially since, often, every nerve in our body screams out "No!"

People often go through bouts of severe depression when they don't have those feelings for God that they once did. They wonder if they were ever "saved." When feelings and emotions pass, it's not time to rev them up again artificially. They will come again on their own, and in their own time. It's time to choose to care about God regardless of your feelings, and trust in His care for you. This is the solid foundation of any lasting and healthy relationship.

9 | A Ramble about Yoda Pancakes

Along with Star Trek, I grew up with Star Wars, Battlestar Galactica, Buck Rogers, and a host of other sci-fi shows of the late '70s and early '80s. My mom was a sci-fi fan and so she introduced me to the ins and outs of hyperspace, warp drive, lightsabers, alien worlds and philosophies, and all the other little impossible or improbable details which makes science fiction so fascinating.

Star Wars has always been one of my favorites. I think the first Star Wars movie I watched in the theater as a kid was The Empire Strike Back. This was the film in which everyone's favorite 900 year old little green Jedi master was introduced, and in which he began to expound more on the Force and the Jedi's interaction with it. One of my favorite sayings from this movie is "No try or try not, Do or Do not, there is no try." Another one of my favorite scenes is when Luke attempts to pull the X-Wing out of the swamp and fails because he believes it's too big. Then Yoda comes up, shakes his head sadly, and proceeds to pull the X-Wing out of the swamp and place it gently on more solid ground. Luke exclaims, "I don't believe it!" To which Yoda replies, "That is why you fail." It's a great lesson on prayer and faith, at least in my opinion.

One of the things that is most amazing about Jedi Master Yoda is how small, how old, and how unassuming he is. When Luke first meets him, he assumes him to be some small, annoying native of Dagobah who seemed to only be there to make his life that much harder. You immediately take a liking to him. Yoda himself seems to be very aware of his size, and his physical inability due to it, but it's not his size that he relies on most. It's the Force.

In the Star Wars universe, the Force is described as an energy field which "binds us, penetrates us, and holds the galaxy together." It's described as the source of a Jedi's power, and the source of all their unique and superhuman abilities. Without it, they can't do anything that a non-Jedi can't do. In using the Force, they are trained from a very young age to interact with it, to use it, and to be used by it in a cooperation and a symbiosis.

In a scene at the end of Attack of the Clones, Yoda displays exactly how adept he is when he uses the Force to stop a massive rock-fall from landing on him by brushing it harmlessly to the side. One thing Yoda never does, however, is take credit for what the Force does. He calls the Force his "ally," and it is clear to him that it is the Force that does all these things. Yoda knows very well that if he attempted any of those amazing things on his own, he'd be in deep, deep trouble.

For example, imagine if Yoda tried to pull the X-Wing out of the swamp on his own. It's likely Luke would have been rolling on the ground laughing as the little Jedi Master got sucked into the bog with the ship. Imagine if Yoda had tried to stop those rocks from landing on himself by just his own strength. You'd have a little green smudge left on the ground; a Yoda pancake. If he tried to do any of it, he would be at best humiliated, at worst, dead.

The normal Christian life, as Watchman Nee called it, is a life lived in cooperation with the Holy Spirit, and under His power and guidance. All the charismata (the gifts of the Spirit) and all the fruit of the Spirit are produced by the Spirit and not through our own natural abilities, no matter how much we try to develop them as qualities within our own lives. There are times God even seems to go out of His way to use people in capacities for which they have no natural ability. All these things are the result of our being joined to Jesus in His death, and cooperating with that death, so that we might be joined with Him in His resurrection. Our natural talents and abilities have nothing to do with it. This tends to be one of the flaws in the popular "spiritual gift tests" which float around Christian circles; a person is likely to answer according to their own natural experience or ability.

Jesus said in John 15 that without Him we could do nothing. If we attempt to live as Christians under our own abilities, then we run the risk of becoming Yoda pancakes. We become self-righteous at best, and it just goes downhill from there. Things like compassion, peace, patience, kindness, goodness, gentleness, and humility are not naturally derived qualities for the Christian. They are produced by remaining in Jesus Christ like the branch remains on the plant, deriving its nourishment from the sap that flows up through the main stalk, trunk, or vine. The charismata (spiritual gifts) such as prophecy, love, faith, mercy, leadership, teaching, etc. are derived from the Spirit, and have nothing to do with a person's training or disciplines. If we attempt them thinking that we're the ones from whom they flow and derive, we run the risk of becoming little green smudges on the ground.

Yoda had the good sense, and eight hundred years of experience as a Jedi, to know how much he wasn't capable of by himself, and this was his truly remarkable feat; his deep humility. We are invited, through Jesus Christ, to partake in the life of the Eternal God and hold an intimate relationship and cooperation with Him. This involves and requires an equally deep humility as He moves within us, through us, and around us. We need to remember at all times that it is Him acting, not us, and in the same way, we need to rely on Him. Through Him mountains can be moved and oceans parted. Without Him we get sucked into the bog and people laugh at us.

10 | A Ramble about Identities

I 've spent more time in meditation lately. I don't know if
anyone has had this experience, but the more time I spend in
meditation, the harder it gets. What I mean is that it seems
to take longer to achieve the point I'm trying to achieve.

In meditation, I've been focusing on pulling away from my "self".
And I've been learning about what that "self" really is. In short, my
"self" is everything I identify myself with. Where I was born, what
I have studied, what my fears are, what my hopes are, even what my
habits are at the grocery store. For example, I identify myself by the
fact that I study Greek. I identify myself by the fact that I am a bit
necrophobic. I identify myself by the fact that whenever I go to the
store I usually pick up a candy bar and/or a drink. I identify myself
by the fact that I'm a priest, a daddy, and a husband, and I identify
myself by my fear of failure. All of these things are facts, and I have
locked on to them for who I believe my "self" to be.

In the Christian life, we are to let all these things go and
identify ourselves with only one thing, the cross of Jesus Christ,
and consequently, His death. I am finding that my own psyche rebels
against this. When I first began to meditate and let go of these other
things that I identify myself with, I had a very physical panic reaction.

As I push for this, and attempt to incorporate letting these things go into my daily life and thought, I find myself psychologically and physiologically stressed. My psyche doesn't want to let go of what it perceives as itself.

The Buddha taught that self was an illusion, that it was nothing more than the aggregation of our minds, bodies, and experiences (more or less, I'm simplifying it here), and that it was the realization of this which led to enlightenment. I'm more and more coming to the opinion that freedom in Christ truly comes only when we fully let go of this illusion of our self, this clinging to certain facts about "this person" for a self-identification. The facts don't change, but we stop allowing them to define who "this person" is. True freedom in Christ comes when we identify with one fact only, His death on the cross.

I say that this is the only fact we may identify with. What about the resurrection? We cannot identify with the resurrection until we have identified with the cross. One cannot resurrect when he hasn't died. To attempt to identify with the resurrection without the cross, without the struggle to let one's "self" go, is a self-delusion. It's the psyche trying to parade itself as renewed and transformed when it is no such thing. The cross means death, and the psyche panics and runs from it in sheer self-preservation when it realizes what the cross really means. It is an act of Grace, and can only be an act of Grace, God's uncreated energy, which enables "this person" to continue on this path of the cross.

It is a true statement that I have died with Christ by being joined to Him through Baptism. The struggle of the Christian life, and our "enlightenment," is the full realization of this fact within our own psyches.

11 | A Ramble about Death

As I've been meditating, I've noticed that while the practice itself is relatively simple, understanding and actually fighting my way through it each day is not. Truth is, I come away feeling a little fried by the end of it. It hasn't, however, been fruitless; just difficult.

This is something I gleaned from it recently: we will either die now, or we will die later. Either we suffer the loss of our selves now, or we will suffer this loss later.

Our intelligence, our experiences, our fears, our desires and appetites, our wealth and possessions, our family and friends -- when we die we lose all of these things. When the physical brain dies, so dies everything housed within it. All that remains is the sense of distinction, the "I and you," between yourself, God, and all other people. Some of this can be seen with Alzheimer's patients, for example.

This will happen whether we choose to cooperate or not. The Path of Jesus Christ is the choice to cooperate with the release of these things now, in this life, in surrender and abandonment to God.

The pain of death comes with the loss of everything we are attached to. In death, these things are consumed before our eyes, and we are drawn back into the love and life of God, retaining the distinction between He and us, but losing all else.

For the worldly person, this process is terrifying. Because of his attachments, as he is drawn into union with God, he goes into Eternal Misery because he refuses to let go. He doesn't want to be united with God, he wants to be an individual ego, and burns with craving for things he can no longer experience. The love of God becomes an eternal torment for that person, as he refuses to accept it.

For the Godly person, this process is welcome, and rest, and returning home as he accepts and enjoys the love and Being of God.

Living the Eternal Life is seeking this release in the here and now by abandoning attachments to one's ego, possessions, and relationships, and becoming one with Christ in His death. As the obstacles to the love of God and union with Him are removed, we realize and experience that we are surrounded and filled with Him, and wrapped and filled with His love. And as this occurs, His love pours out of and through us.

No one comes to the Father without first voluntarily making the cross of Jesus Christ his or her own. No one. No one experiences the life of Jesus Christ without first experiencing His death within themselves; and as His death becomes more and more manifest within us, so then His life becomes more and more manifest within us.

Ultimately we will die, one way or the other. This is the reality of human existence. We can choose to begin the process of letting go of everything now. We can choose to welcome the full experience of God when it comes. We can also choose to lie to ourselves, hang on to everything we can, and then have it all ripped away in eternal misery. It's our choice.

12 | A Ramble about Self-Acceptance

I'm not who I want to be. I'm not who I think I should be. I'm not who I think others want me to be. I'm not who I think others think I should be. As I was meditating today, and saying the Private Mass that has been my daily practice, I struggled and searched for why I have been feeling so cut off lately. Why haven't I been able to experience the Being of God, His love and joy, when He surrounds and fills me and is never apart from me?

I have a real issue with needing the approval or recognition of others. It's funny, because I never really thought I cared about what others thought, but the truth is that what I perceive as others' perceptions about me colors how I perceive myself. As a result, I also have an issue with vanity. Unconsciously I think, "Oh look at me, see now who I am and what I can do. Don't you approve of me now?" And try as I might to fight against it consciously, I seek higher or more prestigious positions. I stress out about how much money I make and how I am presented to others. In other words, I struggle because I identify myself with my perception of other people's perceptions, whether or not my perception is accurate.

As I meditate, a lot of extraneous thoughts come into my mind. My first thought is to reject them. For instance, as I attempted to let go, a scene from the recent Star Trek movie flashed through my mind. It was innocent, and totally benign, but I immediately condemned myself for it happening. I think my unconscious thought was something like, "No, I must reject all of this waste and condemn it."

Now here's the issue: what constitutes all of my identity is effectively that waste. Not that I only or totally identify myself with Star Trek, but it is a part of a larger whole of memories and experiences, preferences, dislikes, hopes, fears, etc, all of which in themselves are quite transient and will eventually be destroyed when this physical being dies. These memories themselves are a mixture of moral, immoral, and amoral constituent parts. Now my rejection of what I see as immoral or waste within me is based on the erroneous idea that the good will be preserved and the bad will be destroyed. In fact, it will all be destroyed upon physical death, and the only thing remaining will be the distinction between God and I, and His all-consuming love.

So here's the answer to my question, "Why do I feel so cut off from God when He surrounds me?" It is because I am projecting my perception of myself onto what I perceive He thinks of me. It seems like this happens on a subconscious level, because with my conscious mind I acknowledge that God loves me, and I Him, and I seek that love, but I allow the darkness which comes from judging myself to obscure my perception of Him.

With God, I have been joined to Jesus Christ in His death and resurrection. This is a fact. All the "waste" has already died, and the wages of sin, being death, are in fact satisfied. The only thing remaining to go is the physical body. He therefore passes no judgment on it because it has already been judged on the cross. That which has died has been freed from sin. He neither indulges it nor condemns it, but accepts it and lets it die peacefully.

This is why I have felt so cut off. I have not accepted my "self" without judgment, nor have I let it die peacefully. I have allowed this lack of acceptance, this non-zero attitude (+1 being indulgence and -1 being condemnation), to be projected onto God and onto others. It erupts into attempts to "prove" how worthy I am, how spiritual, how good, or even how I might be better than the other person, but all the while I am secretly fearful that I am worse than the other person.

Perhaps this is why sin leads to hell, always. And hell doesn't have to be after we die, it is a fact of the living as well as the dead. Sin is a non-zero attitude towards others and ourselves, and it projects our perceptions of ourselves onto everyone else, including and especially God. This perception is fear, whether we know it or not. All the while, God surrounds us with His Being of love. Our ability to recognize that is dependent on our ability to let go of that fear, and stop projecting our perceptions onto Him.

St. Paul said in Romans 8:1 (WEB) – "There is therefore now no condemnation for those who are in Christ Jesus, who don't walk according to the flesh, but according to the Spirit." I think, quite possibly, that this is part of what he meant. Not that God condemns the person in actuality but that we project our own subconscious self-condemnation onto Him; whereas the person who lets the self die peacefully with Christ, neither indulging nor condemning, realizes the ever-present and all-consuming love of God. This person's perception isn't clouded by the darkness of self-judgment.

13 | A Ramble about Blinking Cursors

I'm sitting here staring at a blinking cursor while it expectantly waits for me to come up with something to write, so it can fulfill its purpose in life. It has no other purpose than to tell me where the letters are going to go, and to tell me where it is I'm going to put the next letters I write. It does not praise me when I write nor does it condemn me when I don't, it just waits patiently and expectantly. That is its function, and it is happy to fulfill it. It does not care if what I write is witty. It does not care if it is passionate, intelligent, inane, or dull. It is there to be the instrument of my creativity, and it is happy to do so. It doesn't come up with anything on its own. It waits for me to do that. It only seeks to be my vessel, never going farther than what I intended, nor resisting my input.

If it should decide to print things that I did not type, then it would be malfunctioning and I would have to make corrections involving the delete or backspace key. If it decided not to print things that I did type, then it would be malfunctioning and I would have to find a solution to the problem (generally involving either a reboot, a re-installation, or at worst a new computer). In short, the blinking cursor is humble, obedient, takes no thought for what it wants, and waits to act on my slightest whim.

I'm not a blinking cursor. Sometimes I feel like a blank page, with nothing to say, or not knowing what to say. But I'm not a blinking cursor. I usually have very strong opinions about what should be written, or what shouldn't be. I often write what was not intended, and almost as often don't write what was. I don't wait patiently and expectantly. In short, I am malfunctioning and require at least a reboot on a consistent basis.

It's ironic; if I had to reboot my computer as much as I myself need to be rebooted I would generally either reinstall the software or replace the computer (depending on the issues involved). But I don't get replaced. I haven't gotten reinstalled. I just keep getting rebooted, and I keep getting worked with as is, malfunction and all.

If anyone could judge me, it would be the blinking cursor in front of me. Yet it makes no judgments. I certainly do. This is part of my malfunction. Instead of allowing what should or should not be written to be decided by the Author, I decide for myself what should or should not be written and then I presume to decide it for others as well. This is what was written or not written before, therefore it should be the same every time for every person. I make a poor cursor not permitting the imagination or creativity of the Author.

We can learn a lot about following Christ from just considering the blinking cursor in front of us. He was a good blinking cursor in the Father's hands. He wants us to follow His example.

14 | A Ramble about Broken Things

I had just turned out the light the other night and was getting ready for bed. I then happened to look out my bedroom window onto the parking lot below. There, a few feet from our van, was what looked like an orange light, or some kind of a small fire. It was the oddest thing to see. I didn't have my glasses on, so I couldn't see it very well. I turned this way and that in the window, because I thought it might a reflection on the window from somewhere else in the room, but it stayed where it was. I couldn't figure out what it was, but there it stayed in the parking lot, blazing an orange light with everything that it had.

It bugged me so much that I got out of bed, went down stairs in my bare feet, and went out into the cold, dark, and wet parking lot to find out what it was. I went to the spot where I had seen it from the window and checked it out. Do you know what it was?

It was an old, bent, and broken screw. I looked at it for a while. The head of the screw was still fairly polished, and it had been reflecting the light of the street lamp nearby. It reflected it so well that it looked like someone had left a small fire going in the dark. Now that I think about it, the fact that it was bent at the angle was probably what made it reflect light in my direction so well. If it had been perfectly straight and "useful," not only would it have shone the light in the wrong direction, it might have been more of a danger to the cars that came and went through the parking lot.

There is a prevailing thought, I have heard, that is beginning to wind its way around the Church. This thought is that somehow people can be too broken for the Lord to use, or put in leadership. Somehow, if you have issues or problems in your life, you need to get these in order before you can be of any value to the Church or Christ.

This is utter nonsense. What's worse is that it is totally in contradiction to the clear teachings of Holy Scripture and all precedents therein. The names of broken screws and nuts within the Scriptures are nearly endless: Moses, David, Paul, even Daniel had certain issues (he was probably a eunuch, remember? Just try and tell me that doesn't give someone issues.)

First, God uses those people who are weak, who are foolish, and who are seen as nothing to completely befuddle and put to shame the things of this world. 1 Corinthians 1:26-31 is quite clear about this.

Second, to believe that you are perfectly healthy or OK spiritually, or to believe that you have it all together, is an extremely dangerous place to be and is a hairsbreadth from darkness if you haven't already plunged yourself into it. "Let he who thinks he stands take heed lest he fall."(1 Corinthians 10:12, ESV)

The path of the cross is one of constant admittance that there is something wrong with you. You are malfunctioning. There will be something wrong with you until you die. This is the reality of what St. Paul teaches. You cannot live in the reality of the resurrection until you submit to the reality of the cross. You cannot live until you submit to death.

It does no good for a recovering alcoholic to suddenly say to himself, "Oh, I'm fine, I don't have a problem with this any more." If he does this, and then tells himself one sip won't hurt him, it will be another sip, and then the rest of the bottle. Giving in to "self" is the same way, except far more insidious in that often you don't realize it's happening until it's too late.

God doesn't just use broken things occasionally; they're often the only things God uses. Furthermore, admission of being broken isn't just the beginning of the Path of Jesus Christ, it's the constant guide along it. When you stop following that guide is when you plunge off the Path, and then it can be really hard to find your way back.

1 John 1:8 (WEB) says, "If we say that we have no sin, we deceive ourselves, and the truth is not in us." 1 John 1:10 (WEB) says, "If we say that we haven't sinned, we make Him a liar, and His word is not in us." 1 John 1:9 is a great verse, and comforting when we admit our sin, but we cannot just ignore verses 8 and 10 because we don't want to see them.

15 | A Ramble about What We Ingest

y family and I are on a fairly strict diet. It's Gluten Free, lactose free, and more or less vegetarian. It pretty much consists of rice, beans, fruit, vegetables, and any combination of the first four. It's not as bad as it sounds. We're able to make rice-flour pastas, cakes, and muffins, and it's easier to find gluten free and lactose free foods in a grocery store these days than you might think.

The thing about this kind of a diet is that it supplies what the body needs, and also tends to purge all the other junk from the body. This means that you will probably feel sick for the first month or two (or more) as your system begins to clean itself out of various toxins. If you're like me, you've probably put these toxins in your system for the larger portion of your life eating fast food, TV dinners, and delivery pizzas. Part of this is also going through withdrawals from these kinds of foods and toxins.

But when you've survived and somehow made it out the other side, you tend to actually feel better, you heal faster, and you can have more energy. We went on it out of necessity because my wife is severely gluten intolerant and the rest of us don't do well with gluten or milk either. The downside, in some ways, about going through it is that you lose most or all of your tolerances for the foods that you have given up. Even though I could drink milk or eat cheese before, I can't now because of the effects it has on my stomach and digestive system. And if I break the diet, I tend to feel a little spacey, ill, and like something's just not quite right.

In the writings of the ancient Church and Christian mystics, one of the things they instruct in terms of prayer is to remove all distractions and attachments. The instructions they give at times seem absolutely draconian, such as fasting by eating only once a day, and sleeping only half the night. Withdrawing yourself from most conversations, giving away most or all (preferably all) of your possessions, and drawing all of your attention to your unworthiness, the love of God, and your love for God, is what they lived, taught and encouraged others to follow.

In the course of my reading and meditating I have attempted at least some of what they have prescribed, and during those times of renunciation and removal of myself from distractions such as movies, games, books, etc., things have seemed more "right" spiritually. I was able to let go of "self" more, and spiritual things flowed far more easily. Tears of repentance came far more easily, and His presence was easier to be aware of.

But after some time, I allowed myself to watch a movie, read a book, or play a video game. Nothing truly bad, a little Sci-Fi and some computer games. I've also been reading through the Percy Jackson series. All are fairly benign.

I didn't notice it at first, but the more I did those things, the harder it became to spend time in prayer and meditation. I felt more scattered, and more scattered thoughts intruded into my mind when they weren't wanted. It began with the thought "This couldn't hurt, I did this all the time." But the results were consistent. The more time I spent in prayer, saying Mass, and confining my reading to Scripture and spiritual writings of the Church Fathers and mystics, things began to clear up and flow easier again. The more I watched movies, read other books, and played video games, the harder it became to meditate and pray, and the more I forgot how.

Having a candy bar or some yogurt every once in a while probably won't kill me, but it will throw me off. And if I continue to eat things outside of my diet, it will make me sick and will eventually lead to health problems that could kill me. In the same way, reading a book or watching a movie every once in a while won't completely destroy my relationship with the Lord, neither will He condemn me for it. But the more I ingest that kind of "junk food" the more spiritual health problems I will encounter.

The diet is a pain at times, and it is a bit draconian, but it's there to keep us from getting sick and to heal us from all the other stuff we put into our systems. It's our choice whether or not to follow it, and how strictly, but there will always be consequences for the choices that we make.

16 | A Ramble About Being "in" the World, But Not "of" the World

I've done a lot of talking about what I think Christianity isn't, but I haven't said a whole lot on the subject of what it actually looks like in practice. I go back and look at the spiritual masters of the Church, but most of them were monks either living in communities or solitary. And, as my wife points out, most of them were men, which makes it tough for women to relate to what they're saying. My wife and I talk a lot about this, but the discussion never seems to end with any finality. Most of the discussion centers around this passage found in 1 John 2:15-17:

"Don't love the world, neither the things that are in the world. If anyone loves the world, the Father's love isn't in him. For all that is in the world, the lust of the flesh, the lust of the eyes, and the pride of life, isn't the Father's, but is the world's. The world is passing away with its lusts, but he who does God's will remains forever." (WEB)

A lot of what the earlier saints wrote about was freeing yourself from any and all attachments and distractions which would impede your relationship with God. Those monks out in the desert literally gave away everything they had, and ate only what the body needed to live. They broke off most, if not all, of their family relationships.

They spent large amounts of time in prayer and meditation when they weren't busying themselves with just enough work to be able to feed themselves, or give their wages away.

For one's spiritual health these are probably the ideal conditions of living, because they discipline the body and encourage the person to devote their attention solely to God. Today, churches will often hold retreats that resemble miniature weekend monasteries. They involve few possessions brought of one's own, personal prayer times, and intense communal sessions devoted to prayer and worship. The outside world is shut out so that one can focus on the Lord, free of distractions. But then what happens when one must return to "the real world?"

"The Real World" is full of possessions, movies, music, television programs, books, and relationships with people. In the real world you are constantly bombarded with things that demand your attention and take it away from God, so that the most important relationship professed in your life only gets five to ten minutes a day at best. In "the real world" you have to own several sets of clothing. In "the real world" you have to bring in at least a few thousand a month just to be able to eat, have shelter, and be "normal." In order to reach out to other people in "the real world," you have to be able to relate to them somehow.

Yes, it is possible to pitch the DVDs, books, TV, etc. Yes, it is possible to give away all but the most basic of clothing. Yes, it is theoretically possible to live in this day and age completely isolated from the rest of the world. Some people do. But what about those obligations like spouses, children, and people you care about and who depend on you? What about our obligation to "disciple the nations?" How do we do this in isolation?

I have thrown away my books before (believe it or not). It seems I always acquire new ones. I have given away all of my clothes except for my clerics before. I seem to acquire more of those too. My family and I have gotten rid of most of our furniture and belongings in order to follow where the Lord leads, and both times we received more "stuff" again. What do you do when it doesn't seem like you can even get rid of the "stuff?"

I don't have all the answers; I wish I did. I have a funny feeling that this may look similar yet different for everybody as God works with everyone a little differently, personalizing His treatment plan for each of us, so to speak.

There are a few things, however, that I think we can learn from those monks out in the desert and apply to the lives we have to live in the middle of the world. The first follows from the passage I quoted above, and they centered in on these three things: the lust of the flesh, the lust of the eyes, and the pride of life. These are labeled in the writings of those spiritual fathers as gluttony, avarice or greed, and self-esteem.

In short, they write that these three demons (as they call them) are the forward assault for all other demons to come in and wreak havoc with us. They fasted and ate only what the body needed in order to keep the body under control and keep gluttony at bay. They gave away everything they had and refused to acquire anything more as their own property in order to control their desire to own anything. Self-esteem was the hardest one to keep at bay because it could creep up even, and sometimes especially, when a person was fasting and praying, and could only be fought with tears, the remembrance of our own sins, and the certainty of death.

To allow any of these free-reign opens the door to a downward spiritual spiral. Gluttony, for example, may seem rather benign, but by allowing our body's appetite for food to control us, instead of us controlling it, we set the precedent for ourselves to obey what the body wants to satisfy it. This in turn opens the door for other things, like misplaced sexual desires. In the same way, simply wanting a new dress or a nice pair of shoes seems pretty benign if it doesn't hurt anyone and you can afford it. But it can also open the door to justifying having still more. Self-esteem is often preached from the rooftops and from the pulpits, but the truth is that Jesus taught that we are to crucify ourselves for His sake, and it doesn't take much before we start believing that we "deserve better."

The second thing is how we approach our relationships with other people. Jesus taught that if we loved anyone, and I mean anyone, more than Him, we are not worthy of the Kingdom of

God. Does this mean that we don't care about anyone else? Far from it! But what it does mean is that we have to be aware of our own attachments to other people. Do I depend on my relationship with this person to be happy? Does my self worth depend on how this person sees me? Do I have an attachment to this person that will interfere with my relationship with God? Am I spending more time being aware of my relationship with this person (positively or negatively) than I am being aware of my relationship with God? If the answer is yes to any of these questions, we need to reevaluate that relationship.

All of our relationships with other people must be viewed through our relationship with God, and not vice-versa. For example, I love my wife and children dearly. But I also know that there will come a time when we will all have to say our good-byes and those relationships will end in this life, one way or the other. The loss of those relationships should never be able to damage my relationship with Him. My relationship with God will continue permanently. Just as I must place my relationship with my family as more important than my relationships with co-workers, so must I also place my relationship with God as more important than those relationships with the members of my family.

The third thing I want to address is simply spending time with God and focusing on Him. No relationship can develop unless the two parties spend time with each other and get to know each other. The more time spent, the better the two know each other. The less time spent the less of a chance the relationship has. Be aware of your choices on how you spend your time in this matter.

Finally, we must simply be aware of the choices we make and the consequences thereof. We must always keep in mind that we were born naked, and we will die with less than that. When we die, we will have only our relationship with God, or lack thereof. Everything else in this life is either a help or a hindrance to that relationship, depending on how it's used. If you can live in this world with possessions, family, friends, etc. and be free from the distractions and attachments that impede your relationship with God, more power to you. If you need to give everything away and live as a hermit in the desert in order to draw closer to Him, then do it. Most of us will probably fall somewhere in between, but we need to be aware of when we believe we can't do without something of this world, or if it seems more important than Him. It may then be time to rethink our priorities.

17 | A Ramble about Freedom in Christ

There is a lot of talk about having freedom in Christ among the various churches and in various sermons. But, as I was thinking about it this morning during prayer, I don't think it means what a lot of people take it as.

First, Freedom in Christ has nothing whatsoever to do with doing whatever you want and getting away with it. Often, the message comes across as freedom in Christ being equated with freedom from law, from discipline, from consequences, etc. But nowhere does it ever teach this concept in the New Testament; in fact, it teaches quite the contrary. As St. Paul writes in Romans 6:1-2, "Should we continue to sin that grace may abound? Absolutely not, how can we who died to sin live any longer in it?"

Freedom in Christ is about freedom from self, freedom from the slavery to possessions, and freedom from slavery to one's passions and carnal inclinations. It's about the world being crucified to you, and you to the world. The person who is still enslaved to his porn habit, the person who can't stop smoking because his body demands it, the person who feels like he always has to have more and more, the person who loves to get up on stage and hear people clap for him – these people haven't found freedom in Christ, but are still slaves to their own disorder, and will be so until they embrace the death of the cross.

Freedom comes at a price. This is the lesson of American history. That price is almost always paid in blood, as well as sweat and tears. Freedom in Christ is no different. He paid it in blood so that we don't have to be enslaved to ourselves, but that we might live for Him who died for us. In order to truly realize that freedom in Him we have to do the hard work of abandoning ourselves, letting go of all those things which enslave us, and embracing His death as our own. Then, and only then, will we truly experience that freedom.

18 | A Ramble about Career Students

"You search the Scriptures because you think that in them you have eternal life; and it is they that bear witness about me, yet you refuse to come to me that you may have life." (John 5:39-40, ESV)

There comes a point in time when you just have to put your Bible down. Your Bible, your devotionals, your study guides, all of it. There's nothing wrong with studying the Scriptures and attending Bible studies. These things are good, especially to one who is new to the faith. But, there comes a point in time when you have to stop hiding behind the facade of learning about your faith, and start doing what your faith says to do. It is good to memorize scripture in order to keep your mind focused on where it belongs. It isn't good to continuously study on the pretext of learning something "more."

There are people who attend college with a certain goal, a vocation, in mind. They go, they get their education, and then they go on to be teachers, doctors, lawyers, nurses, engineers, and so on. Then there are people who attend college to learn, but continue to attend because they're afraid of life. Once they graduate, they attend still more college and become career students. They don't enter the outside world partly because they're fascinated by learning more, but even more because they're afraid of the outside world and doing what it is they've been taught to do.

There are too many Christians who do the same thing. "Getting in the Word," going to church, and going to Bible study groups are all about remaining in the classroom without having to actually employ what it is they learn there. There is a time and a place for the classroom, and the classroom mentality, but we weren't meant to never venture outside of it.

The gathering of the faithful to worship on Sunday mornings (or whatever time and day of the week it may be) is just that; a time to worship and remember the covenant God made with us through the body and blood of Jesus Christ. It is a time to gather together as the body, worshiping together as the body of Christ. Quite frankly, it really isn't a time for yet more basic classroom instruction. Yet all too often this is what it has devolved into, to the point where the worship and remembrance has taken a back seat to between 30 and 60 minutes of theological exposition and speculation by the minister. In most non-sacramental churches today, the typical service looks something like this: fifteen minutes of hymns, five minutes of announcements, forty-five minutes of sermon, Holy Communion once a month.

There comes a point in time when you have to step outside of the classroom and use what you have learned instead of hiding in the classroom. What good is a soldier who never ventures into combat? What good is a farmer who never works his fields? What good is a doctor who has never diagnosed a patient?

The Bible itself is a tool. It cannot do the work of discipleship for you. The Bible is, at the end of the day, a printed book that carries a message. The message must be internalized and put into practice or else reading it cover to cover repeatedly, studying it in minute detail, and memorizing it word for word will do you no good.

At the end of the day, if it doesn't lead you back to Jesus, even studying the Bible is for nothing.

19 | A Ramble on Cleaning Toilets

Would you be willing to clean the Lord's toilets for eternity if He told you to? Cleaning toilets is humiliating work, especially if that's all someone thinks you're good for. But what if that's what the Lord decided he wanted you to do for Him? Personally, I can't handle humiliation well. I've never been able to. I can't handle watching other people being humiliated, and I've never handled my own humiliation well.

But humiliation is what we're called to since we are called to imitate our Lord. He Himself stripped down to His underwear to wash the dirt, toe jam, and street feces off of His disciple's feet because no one else would do it. It's humiliating work. So is cleaning toilets.

Humiliation fights against our self-esteem and shows us some of the worst feelings in ourselves, just like a good 360 degree mirror shows us all the flaws in our body shape that we don't want to notice. We try to cover and hide it with well-cut clothing. The truth is that humiliation can be one of the most potent tools for growth towards realization of our Union with Him, but it is also one of the most painful. It has the capability of encouraging us to empty ourselves, but it also has the capability of destroying us to the point of psychosis. Only God knows how far it can safely be taken with each one of us.

I had to clean toilets in Bible School. I had to clean them at several of the places where I worked. I've gotten to the point where it doesn't bother me that much anymore. But it still humiliates me when it seems like that's all people think I'm capable of. It's painful. Having a cancer removed is painful too. Both can be necessary in order to be healed.

20 | A Ramble about the Man in the Mirror

ome time ago the late king of pop, Michael Jackson, sang "I'm looking at the man in the mirror, I'm asking him to change his ways . . . If you want to make the world a better place take a look at yourself and make a change . . . " (*Man in the Mirror*) Whatever you may think of the song's author, he made a good point with it.

Jesus told us at the end of the Gospel of Matthew, "As you go, disciple all the nations, baptizing them in the name of the Father, and of the Son, and of the Holy Spirit, teaching them to observe everything whatsoever I commanded you . . . " (Matthew 28:19; my translation from the Greek text)

There are times when I keep feeling, "I'm ready to do this," and I get depressed at not being in a good position to go out and teach others the things I've learned. I watch friends that I went to school with go on and pastor churches or go out to foreign missions, and they all seem to be doing everything I wanted to do with my life.

"What then would I teach, and who would listen?" I asked myself this morning. "Well, I would teach people about Christ and how to follow him." I answered. "Really, do you follow Him?" I asked myself. "Are you doing everything He taught? Are you really a disciple? Do you practice what you preach? More importantly, do you practice what He preached?"

It is necessary to send people to preach the Gospel to those who have never heard it, but it is even more necessary for those of us who profess to follow Christ to actually do it. The first person I must make a disciple of is myself, and no one else can do it for me.

It is the man in the mirror that I must first disciple for Christ. It is the man in the mirror that I must first equip to follow Him. I must convince this man who stares back at me of the truth of the Gospel first. Then, and only then, when he has understood it and internalized it and put it into practice will he be ready to disciple anyone else. And, I'm just not that great of a judge as to when he'll actually be ready for it.

Being a Christian is about far more than going to church on Sundays, saying the right things, and telling yourself you believe the right things. It's about putting the life of Jesus Christ into practice, and that takes practice. It takes weathering constant subtle and not so subtle attacks from forces both seen and unseen. It takes acquiring humility, self-control, and yes, a voluntary poverty (as in not letting "things" control you) regardless of how much you own. Most often, it also takes time. There are some that are given the Grace to breeze right through. The rest of us have to slog through it step by painful step with the Grace He allows us, to keep us from flying too high too fast and subsequently falling too far too hard.

It all starts with a heart to heart conversation with the man in the mirror, just like M.J. said.

21 | A Ramble about Hatred

What is hatred itself? If love is the choice to positively or benevolently care about someone no matter what they do or how they make you feel, then hatred is the opposite. It is the choice to negatively or malevolently care about someone no matter what they do or how they make you feel. It is the choice to cause or will harm to that person actively or passively.

Have you ever considered that the act of hating someone, especially in holding a grudge against them, has nothing to do with the person you are hating? Hatred is like trying to hit a moving target. As soon as you lock on to the person to hate, they change and are no longer the same person.

We hate the person who wronged us, usually, in some way. We hate what that person did. But consider that the image or perception of the person becomes imprinted in our mind. We cannot think of the person in question without bringing up that perception. The person himself or herself however never remains in the same place they were when they did the wrong. They change, they grow or get worse as the case may be, but the person whom you have locked onto in order to hate is gone forever.

All too often, we don't actually feel a certain way towards the actual person, be it love or hatred, but rather we feel a certain way towards our perception of that person. This can be easily seen with fans of celebrities. They learn about the person, memorize details about a person, fantasize about the person, and love the person dearly all without actually having met the person in question. And often, when they do, they are confronted with someone whom they don't know, and are thus often crushed.

For this reason, hatred is pointless when directed towards any human being, and only hurts the innocent, never the guilty party. If you consider that the perception of the person which we hate is really a projection of our own minds, then we are in actuality only hating that projection of our minds and the memory of the event or emotion associated with the hatred. We then misdirect that hatred towards the actual person in question. The person in question often has nothing to do with the hatred he or she encounters from us. Hatred begins within the hater, and it is only within the hater that it can be fought. Directing more hate towards the person who hates us does not end the hatred, but only causes us to be caught hating that perception of the hater and thus that part of our own minds.

The Buddha taught that hatred cannot be appeased with hatred, but hatred can only be appeased with "not-hatred." Jesus Christ taught "But I say to you, Love your enemies and pray for those who persecute you, so that you may be sons of your Father who is in heaven. For he makes his sun rise on the evil and on the good, and sends rain on the just and on the unjust." (Matthew 5:44-45, ESV) And St. Paul taught "Repay no one evil for evil, but give thought to do what is honorable in the sight of all. If possible, so far as it depends on you, live peaceably with all. Beloved, never avenge yourselves, but leave it to the wrath of God, for it is written, 'Vengeance is mine, I will repay, says the Lord.' To the contrary, 'if your enemy is hungry, feed him; if he is thirsty, give him something to drink; for by so doing you will heap burning coals on his head.' Do not be overcome by evil, but overcome evil with good." (Romans 12:17-21, ESV)

We must in fact save our hatred for those things that truly deserve it. We must wish deliberate harm on the disorder that so easily causes us to harm ourselves and others. Hatred is well deserved for things within ourselves like ignorance, violence, abusiveness of any kind, malice inflicted on others, and all such things as this. Hatred can be a powerful tool for spiritual growth if I unleash it on my own disorder and let it wreak havoc with my own complacency, pride, greed, selfish ambitions, and lack of self-control; as long as I do not misdirect it at the person who is afflicted with these things. I must let it attack the disorder itself.

22 | A Ramble about Conditioning

I don't know about anyone else, but I liked the *Karate Kid* remake with Will Smith's kid in it. I grew up with the original Ralph Machio versions, and even liked *The Next Karate Kid* with Mr. Miyagi teaching Hillary Swank. Yes, this shows my age, but hey, it was cool then, and it's cool now.

In the remake, instead of the "wax on, wax off" routine, a Chinese Miyagi, Mr. Han (played so well by Jackie Chan), has "Dre" (the remake's Daniel) simply pick up his jacket, hang it up, take it off, put it on himself, take it off, drop it on the floor, and repeat. Over, and over, and over again. Now, keep in mind, Mr. Han is supposed to be teaching Dre the Chinese martial art, Kung Fu. This is something Dre reminds him of, many, many times. After the thousandth time or so, Dre gets fed up, and demands to know what it is that he's learning from hanging up his jacket a thousand times. After the outburst, where some choice things were said towards Mr. Han, Mr. Han comes over and proceeds to show him what he has learned, retooling the simple movements of bending down, throwing the jacket over the shoulders, and throwing it on the peg into defensive movements that block punches and kicks. He did it a thousand times, and without knowing it, his body memorized those movements so that when they were re-purposed for something else, his body responded without him thinking about it. Without him knowing it, Mr. Han had conditioned his body to respond in a certain way. All by repeating the same boring movements over and over again.

This is what martial artists must do from the time they start. They take one movement and practice it over and over and over until their bodies do it without having to think about it, a thousand times, two thousand times. It's boring, it's time consuming, it's hard work, and it doesn't seem to have any short-term goal or benefit. But it's crucial that the body master the movement. This is the essence of what the term "Kung Fu" means; mastery of a skill derived from hard work and study.

My wife and I have often asked God, "Why do we constantly go through the same thing over and over again?" Recently, we thought we had learned the lesson we needed to and expected things to move to the next level, but no, things continue as they were. Here we are again. And we ask, "Why?"

When God teaches us and trains us, it isn't like the classes and tests we take in school. There, we absorb information and are expected to spit it back out on a test. Once we can do this reasonably well, we move on to the next level. God trains us more like a martial arts sensei or sifu. He makes us do the same simple thing over and over again, not just until we get it right, but until we can do it without thinking; until it becomes a part of how we live, move, and breathe. He doesn't just teach us, He conditions us.

This is why it seems like we have to learn the same lesson over and over again. It's not that we don't know it. It's that it hasn't been fully incorporated into our very being yet. Where faith and love are concerned, where prayer and dependence on God are concerned, where letting go of everything else and forgiving are concerned: these aren't lessons that you can just squeak by with a C- in the class. These are foundational movements that must be practiced over and over and over again.

So, as long as we still have to think about it, God will continue to make us pick up our jackets, hang them up, take them off, put them on, take them off, drop them on the floor, and repeat, until we do it without thinking. This is the path of a disciple. If we leave off to go and do something else for a while thinking that we've learned what we needed to, when we come back we're back to doing the same thing we left off at, over and over and over again.

23 | A Ramble about Spiritual Exercises

Some time ago, I worked at a facility for troubled teenage boys. Their troubles ranged anywhere from having anger issues to having committed murder, from being raped to being the rapist. Some were just kids who hadn't been given a chance, others were truly disturbed mentally and emotionally. It was a job that wasn't for everyone, and could be extremely stressful since you never knew what was going to happen next, or whether some kid was going to try and severely hurt you or kill you.

Under it all however, they were all crying out, in their own ways, to be cared about and to have positive attention paid towards them. I realized that working there, at least for me, required a kind of spiritual discipline that had to be adhered to. Jesus taught to bless those who curse you. I was called various profane names every five minutes, and often wondered if I was doing something wrong if I wasn't. Jesus taught to do good to those who hate you. I was told I was hated, verbally and non-verbally, from the time I started my shift to the time they went to bed at night. Jesus taught to love your enemies. I was seen as their enemy just by virtue of the fact I was staff and followed the guidelines, no matter what I did.

When I later worked at another facility, this one in the girls house, I took that understanding with me. I was fortunate that the girls weren't quite so aggressive, but again it required the same spiritual discipline. In the girl's house I was scratched by nails dug deep into my skin, bitten frequently, punched, and my nose was broken once from a head butt. Jesus taught to love your enemies. He taught to forgive, and you will be forgiven. He taught that God is good even to the ungrateful and to the wicked, and so I was to emulate Him and be as much of a father to those girls as He was to me.

I can't say I exercised that spiritual discipline perfectly. I didn't. I failed. I got stressed out. I did and said things I shouldn't have more frequently than not. But that's the thing about a discipline, it assumes that you aren't finished yet, and it's there to teach you and shape you closer to the end result.

There are a great many spiritual disciplines and spiritual exercises in the Christian tradition. Most of these come from the monastic traditions and involve fasting, chastity, poverty, humility, prayer and meditation; all of which are good and healthy for spiritual growth, but cannot be allowed to become an end of themselves, or else they are self-defeating. The true spiritual discipline is as our brother St. Paul says:

"Therefore I urge you, brothers, by the mercies of God, to present your bodies a living sacrifice, holy, acceptable to God, which is your spiritual service [latreia]." (Romans 12:1, WEB, brackets added) This spiritual service, in the Greek "latreia", literally means the kind of service which a priest (in the Temple) provided at the altar or in the execution of his priestly office.

The spiritual exercises that count are those that we practice from moment to moment and in every decision we make. They occur in our daily routine and how we respond to other people, no matter who it is. Do we put how the other person feels above how we feel? If someone steals from me, do I prosecute him? If someone hits me, or abuses me, do I strike back? Do I put how my wife feels over and above my own physical desires? Do I accept a rebuke without comment? Do I cry out for the Grace of God in my own heart where no one but He and I can see, or do I proudly march forward into waiting temptations only to fail? Am I so afraid of not having enough? Do I only trust in what I can see, so that I hoard money, food or possessions? Do I give to those who ask, or do I turn them away?

These kinds of things are where the rubber meets the road, and these are the tests and exercises that we must face every day and which really matter. The prayers and liturgies which we recite help in crying out to Him and in activating that ever present Grace, but they can never take the place of the true disciplines which move us forward towards our goal.

24 | A Ramble about Gardening

We've finally gotten our gardens in over the last couple of months. The house we're living on is situated in the middle of what has consistently been fertile, well producing farmland; some of the best in this area. Every year it still produces fields of good crops of wheat or peas for the farmers that rent this land from my in-laws. It's so fertile that, in a good year for rain, you literally just have to throw the seed over it and it grows with little more done to encourage it.

It's funny how I'd forgotten that I actually enjoy farming or gardening. I took horticulture and agriculture classes in high school and they were some of the few classes that I actually looked forward to when I was in school. I enjoyed the feel and smell of the soil, especially when it was just watered. I don't remember being very good at it, a lot of which had to do with my being a teenager at the time, but I do remember looking forward to that part of the day.

There are several things that are coming back to me as I'm doing this with my wife. The first is that it's hard work. There's really no way around it being hard work. There are ways to make it less hard, but not by much. My back has now put me on its "do-not-call" list.

It doesn't want to know that I need to get back out there and use the hoe, and when it learns about it my back protests loudly.

The second is that you have to be careful with how much of anything that you give it. There's a danger in both giving it too little water and too much. There's a danger in both giving it too little fertilizer and too much. Too little water and the plant dies from being too dry. It just shrivels up. Too much and it dies from drowning in it. This happened with our first batch of tomato plants because of the deluge of rain that we got this past spring. Too little fertilizer and the plant may not have the nutrients it needs to grow right and produce fruit. Too much and it will burn the plant's roots and kill it completely. Too little sun and it can't produce chlorophyll, too much sun and it'll dry out the soil too fast. It's got to be moderate amounts of each. Not too much, and not too little.

The third is that you have to pull up weeds when they're small. You'd think this would be a no-brainer, but the truth is that when weeds are small, they don't look like much of a threat. But if you leave them alone, they grow faster than you expect and put down deep roots quickly. Then when they are an obvious threat they are much more labor intensive to remove, and some are nearly impossible without damaging the plants you want to keep.

The seed and soil have to be good too. If there's something wrong with the seed, it may not grow at all no matter what you do to encourage it. Not every kind of seed grows the same way either. You have to be patient with pepper seed, and they have to be planted under certain conditions with the right temperatures. Whereas with beans, every second grader knows you can plant them in a paper towel and Ziploc bag and they'll grow just fine. If the soil's got too much clay, there won't be enough drainage. If it's got too little, there will be too much. It seems like seed grows really well in the decaying remains of other plants, whereas chemical fertilizers may do nothing at all or hurt it. Some seed will grow just fine on the surface of the soil, other seed needs to be planted a little deeper before it germinates.

It's no secret that Jesus and St. Paul often used farming and gardening as a metaphor for spiritual growth. One of the best known parables is the "Parable of the Sower." A sower is a person that goes out and spreads seed over a tilled field by throwing it out and letting it land where it will.

Jesus explained that the seed was His message, and the different kinds of ground where the seed fell were the different kinds of people who received the message. I think that the metaphor can be taken to include some of the lessons learned from literal gardening.

First, spiritual growth is work. It is hard work, and don't let anyone con you into thinking otherwise. It requires constant weeding, watering, feeding, and guarding your crop so that various wild animals don't come in and steal or damage the fruit. I can't stress enough that you can't let down your guard for even a moment.

Second, you have to be moderate in everything. Too much of anything physically or spiritually will damage your spiritual growth. Too much food, sex, or sleep no matter how innocuous it may seem will get you hooked on those sensual desires and fling open the doors for other more dangerous demons (literal or figurative, take your pick) to rampage in and destroy you. Too little and your body begins to starve, become delirious, and becomes far more easily tempted to over-indulge. You must allow the right moderation of each, as much as Grace allows, and no more. The same is true of spiritual things. Too much prayer, scripture, or even sacrament too soon and it can be damaging because it can lead to self-esteem, and then the far more deadly error of pride. Too little prayer, scripture, or sacrament and you won't have enough of the nutrients you need to grow spiritually. You must learn, whether it is physically or spiritually, to take only what you need to grow and be sustained for the day. Neither more, nor less, because any suggestion to take more or less is not from God, but from your own demons and desires which want to get as far from God as possible.

Third, you have to stop desires when they're small, even if they don't look like any kind of a threat. Notice, I didn't say "sinful" desires. The three desires, or demons, which open the gateway for all the others are gluttony (or a lack of self-control), avarice (otherwise known as greed), and self-esteem. Gluttony for our purposes means being immoderate with anything your physical body needs. This is hard because it could be something as simple as, "Well, it's just one more candy bar." Or it could be, "Let me sleep in just another fifteen minutes," or "Just one look won't hurt" (you know what I'm talking about). The body needs food. Too little, and it dies too soon; too much and it grows obese and dies too soon. The body has a sex drive (yes, this differs from person to person). Too little and a person suffers psychologically and emotionally, too much and they become a slave to it. The body needs sleep. Too little and you start seeing funny pink elephants with white polka-dots, too much and it starts being unable to function. Avarice can seem to be as innocuous as "Oh, that would look great on me!" Or, "If I only made another fifty cents an hour," or "If I made more money I would be able to help more people." This last one is quite dangerous because it opens the door to the desire to have more through the excuse of wanting to help others, and then shifts the focus to just having more and little by little forgetting about others. Self-esteem is insidious and dangerous and can work either positively or negatively. It starts with, "Well, I'm a pretty good person," or "Well, at least I'm not like that person." Inversely it can be "I can't believe I did that, I'm such a horrible person." It's the desire to be, or not be as the case may be. If you don't recognize and stop these things when they are small, they will grow quickly and spiral out of control. Then, finding them and uprooting them becomes a much harder, more painful, and intensively laborious task that may prove to be impossible without help.

Finally, the message has to be the right one. If you haven't been planted with Jesus Christ Himself, with the gospel and message He taught, with the life and path He walked; don't be surprised if the crop you get is deformed, doesn't produce fruit, or doesn't grow at all. If your life doesn't start to look like Jesus or His Apostles, check your seed, check the soil that it's planted in, and then check for weeds which could be choking your growth.

There are some people that garden just for a hobby. It's something to do just to entertain themselves and keep busy. There are others who garden because they need to eat and feed themselves. There are some people that profess faith and are baptized just because it's "the thing to do." There are others who do so because they truly want union with God. What is your goal with your faith and practice? Is it just some kind of a hobby? Or are you serious about the final goal of union with God? Are you serious about producing fruit in your garden, or is it just there for fun and left to overgrow when it gets boring? St. Paul, in Philippians 3 gave his answer. He wrote that he had suffered the loss of everything in order that he might obtain Christ, and that he counted everything else as trash. Jesus compared it to a treasure buried in a field for which a man sold everything he had just to buy the field it was in. How important is your garden to you? How important to you is it that it produces fruit?

25 | A Practical Manual to Following the Path of Jesus Christ

An ancient manual of Christian practice, called the Didache, said there were two ways: the way of life and the way of death. Two paths to follow.

The path of life is the path of Jesus Christ. The path of death is the path of self. The path of Jesus Christ is the path of love, of caring, and of compassion. The path of death is the path of selfishness, of fear, of hoarding, of insecurity, of anger, and of hatred.

The only way to experience God in practice is by choosing to care about someone else, and forgetting about yourself or your own wants, needs, and desires *in that moment*. If you don't forget about these things, they will form a barrier between you and Him.

Love, caring, compassion; the choice to put someone else's interests above your own is the catalyst. It allows Grace to flow through you like power through circuits. It allows you to step back and become one with God in such a way that you become almost an observer in your own body as you see what He does through you. And when He does this, your concern for the other person intensifies and they become the most important thing to you *in that moment*, whether it's your dearest friend, or the person who just broke your nose or gave you a black eye. And it has nothing to do with your feelings. It is the simple yet powerful choice to set anything about you aside and focus on the other person.

Jesus commanded us to love. There's a reason for it. He commanded us to make the choice to care, because this, through Him, is our salvation. It allows the union with Him to take place in practice. It doesn't matter who the object of that concern is. It can be the bum on the street, the cashier at the supermarket, your family, your friends, the person who hates you and despises you, or God Himself; and it must be each one of these people in turn. The power to do so is there by Grace, and by means of love Grace itself is made active and perfected.

There are two paths, and they are mutually exclusive. You cannot practice love *and* be continuously concerned for your own "self." It doesn't work that way. If you leave room for yourself it throws up a barrier to love. If you choose (and it is a choice) to worry only about your health, your wealth, your fortunes, your wants and desires, your notions, and your ideas, then it throws up a barrier to love; and consequently to God Himself and union with Him. If you choose to love, you throw yourself to the winds and embrace the other person. You can't do both.

Here is how it works. You pray and ask God for Him to love the other person through you. You then choose to focus on this person, and make them your only concern *in that moment*. You hold on to this. You don't let it go. You willfully forget or ignore your own needs or pains or interests at that time. You will be surprised to discover how easy it becomes when you let go of your fears about it. And you will then experience saying and doing things that don't originate with you, but come about through your actions and words; and the words coming out of your mouth will teach you as well.

This works no matter who the object of your love may be, with the exception of yourself (unless you treat yourself as a third party, and then only sparingly). When you are with friends, practice it. When you are with someone who despises you, practice it. When you are by yourself, remember that God surrounds you and is within you, and practice it with Him. When you are with a total stranger, practice it. And when you practice it, you will be one with Him. And the more you practice it, the easier it will become.

Focus on nothing else. Nothing else is worth focusing on. Why try to live as long as you can? You will die anyway. Why try to gain more money or a better position in life? You will lose them one way or another. You cannot lose this union except by selfishness. Sell everything you have figuratively – and literally if need be – to acquire it, and you won't be disappointed. As you enter into this union with Him by love you realize, as He loves the other person through you, how much He loves you as well; and you know that this does not change, because He doesn't change. He is stationary, static, and unmoving. His love is permanent, and does not move as He does not move.

Everything else, anything else, really doesn't matter as long as you work on this. Master this and you master everything because you are in God and God is within you.

26 | The Lesson of the Watermelon Plant

There is in our garden a watermelon plant that, by all rights, should be dead. We planted it when we planted the squash and the cantaloupe. At the beginning of the season, the squash and the cantaloupe began to grow slowly but surely. But no matter what we did with the watermelon, it just kept looking more and more unhealthy. It withered up and kept only a few dry leaves. The stem split in two right down the middle near the base of the plant. It didn't matter how much water I gave it. It didn't matter if I let it go a day or two. It looked so pathetic I seriously considered just pulling it up and being done with it. But something inside me just kept saying, "Just give it another day. Water it today . . . " I felt so sorry for it that I did just that.

Then, out of the blue, it started growing and producing a few flowers. It just kept growing and growing, and now it has a good-sized watermelon growing on it. We tried to bind the stem together, but it's still cracked down the middle. The stem is so hard and woody that you wouldn't believe it was alive at all, much less that it was a part of the same plant. Truth is I have no idea why this plant is still alive, much less why it's bearing fruit. The only explanation I have for it is that God told it to.

I know there's a lesson in this somewhere. There are probably several lessons to learn from it. Not all of our plants have survived. The garlic we planted, which started out well, has completely died. The chives are barely holding on. The pepper seeds we planted in nice neat little rows never came up. Those rows are completely barren, and I have no explanation as to why they didn't at least germinate. But this watermelon plant that looked like it was dead shortly after we planted it is now growing and bearing fruit.

You never know which seeds will grow when you plant them, no matter how much you take care of them. You never know which plants will live and which will die, and it won't always make sense when they do. It will frustrate you no end to realize that you really have no control over it at all.

We want the seeds of faith to grow where we plant them. We want the people we spend time with and care for to grow and bear fruit in the way we want. We want to be able to spread the Gospel and have whole fields of people respond and grow as we water and weed them. Our watermelon plant and our garlic plants say it doesn't work that way. The Scriptures say that one person plants, another waters, but it is God who makes it grow, not the person working the garden (see 1 Corinthians 3:6-9).

God makes all plants grow as it pleases Him. Sometimes He chooses to let the plant grow immediately. Sometimes, He chooses for it to not grow at all. Sometimes, He chooses to take mercy on a plant that is almost dead. Sometimes He lets a plant that looked like it was healthy die on its own. We have no control over this. The only thing we can do is keep planting seed, watering it, and weeding it carefully where it won't hurt the plant's growth.

Part IV | God

1 | The Love of God

God's love is who He is. When we interact with God, we interact with His love. Whether we are experiencing the bliss of Eternal Life or the fires of Gehenna, whether we are comforted in our sorrow, rebuked in our errors, or purged through fire, we are encountering the love of God. The only thing that changes throughout all of these experiences is us, and how we perceive Him and encounter His love. This all-penetrating, all-consuming love surrounds, fills, and penetrates us, because *He* surrounds, fills, and penetrates us. God has no other mode of operation. He is love.

Why then can we experience Hell? Because of His love. The Fires of Gehenna are what we experience when all we encounter is this all consuming, devastating Love, and instead turn towards physical and transient cravings and desires that leave one continuously craving for more. The fires of Gehenna are what we experience when we refuse to let go of our fears and delusions of control and just accept His all-consuming love on His terms. His all-consuming devastating love for us is also an all-consuming devastating hatred for the sin malfunction that afflicts every one of us, in the same way that the parent of a child with a disorder loves that child fiercely while at the same time curses and fiercely hates the child's affliction.

God does not move, we do. His love does not move; it is always there because He is always there. Why then do we not always feel it? The answer is that we do, but do not always understand what we are feeling. Or we ignore it for the impermanent and relatively meaningless things our senses are telling us. We don't slow down long enough to pay attention to what is right in front of us.

The Love of God feels harsh at times, just like my love for my children feels harsh to them when they disobey. I hate their disobedience because I love them fiercely and I have a particular vision of the kind of people they can be if not for their disobedience. I want them to always experience my love in a positive way, but that depends on their perception, and I know that my love can't waver even if they have a misperception of it.

The love of God is purifying, and it can be painful in its purification as it burns away everything we still grasp for and crave. This is why a time of purging and a state of hell often feel the same; the difference between them is our response to this devastating and terrible Love. The difference between a purging and damnation is literally whether we are willing to surrender to the Love of God and let go of all else or not.

He rages because He is love. He burns away all that we desire because He is love. He hates because He is love. He is still, unmoving, uncompromising, and unwavering because He is love. He comforts, encourages, pushes us onwards, and is unrelenting because He is love.

The love of God is devastating, terrible, and terrifying in its power, scope, and absoluteness. In the face of such love, we can either surrender and be enraptured and consumed by it, or be destroyed with all else we cling to.

2 | A Ramble about the Humility of God

Recently, as I struggled through meditation, I found it harder and harder to reach the point of awareness of His presence. I fought through, but each time it became harder, and for several weeks it seemed completely fruitless. I struggled, cried out internally, and . . . nothing.

I felt lost and confused. Why had He slipped through my fingers when I reached out to grasp Him? Didn't He want me coming closer to Him? Where was He? I knew He surrounded me, I knew that He was in everything and everywhere and that there was nowhere I could go where He was not. So why did I feel so cut off?

He told me.

I sought control of Him. I sought the awareness of His presence in order to change myself into something "better." I sought union with Him to advance my own twisted reason and to satisfy my fear of being "less than" with the offering of being "better than" spiritually. He refused to be a part of my self-seeking and self-advancement. It was as simple as that.

I have a deep seated fear that everyone else is better than I am in some way, and my psyche seems to react by trying to, consciously or unconsciously, be better than everyone else. I seek to control and manipulate everything around me to achieve the acquisition of my own desires or illusions, whether it be the desire for a certain object such as a DVD or book, or the illusion of seeing myself as a good or spiritual person. I sought to run from what I am, and to become something I am not. Instead of accepting myself as myself, warts and all, I was rejecting myself in favor of a pleasant delusion. Instead of embracing the cross, I was running from it while yelling, "I embrace you!"

When I realized this, I sat in silence. And then I became aware of His presence. It was not imposing. He was not overwhelming. He was quiet. He was soft and gentle. He was concerned, and it felt as when a friend of mine was giving me a hug from behind. As I dwelt on this I became aware of the stark contrast between Him and myself and the disdain which this controlling part of myself felt for His "softness." This part of me was hard, proud, dominating, and the total antithesis of Him. It honestly didn't know what to do with Him. God in this manner did not force Himself on me, but waited for me to sit still. He did not strike me as awe-inspiring, but "lowly."

God felt no need to prove or show His dominance to me. Almighty God was as soft and gentle as, well . . . a small animal. I don't know why, but that is the term that comes to mind. I wanted the awareness of the presence of God, and instead of awe-inspiring power, I got soft and gentle like someone's toothless old great-grandfather.

As I said above, this hard controlling part of me didn't know what to do with it. It felt, well . . . pathetic actually, and totally non-controlling, even though I knew He had full control of everything. And then my thoughts drifted onto His humility. It's not an aspect of God that we often think about or preach on.

He surrounds us constantly, yet most of the time makes no visible effort to remind us of that fact. We often ignore Him far more than anyone else and talk about Him as if He weren't in the room with us. Even we who profess not only belief and faith in Him but also love, often go whole days without even noticing Him or acting as if He were present. He doesn't respond in anger. He doesn't seek to prove how much better than we are He is. He lets us go, and takes no offense. He who has ultimate control chooses not to wield it in that way. And here I, who have no real control over anything, am seeking to control Him for my own selfish means.

I suppose that the real first step in any relationship is to truly notice the other person, instead of going throughout the day pretending that they don't exist except for your own selfish goals. It's to really see them for who they are, and not for what you can get out of them.

Unlike myself, God is totally devoid of pride and selfish ambition. When I became aware of His presence in this way, I realized how truly ridiculous and maligning my own hardness was, especially to Him.

3 | A Ramble about Change and Perception

It is a stated fact that God Himself doesn't change. Some theologians or would-be theologians would probably debate this, but He doesn't. He says as much within Sacred Scripture. "For I the LORD do not change; therefore you, O children of Jacob, are not consumed." (Malachi 3:6, ESV)

Think about what this means for a minute. God Himself is static. He doesn't move. Change happens around Him, within Him, and through Him. But He Himself remains motionless, still, and we and the flow of time move and change along His quiet surface like the ripples over a pond. God doesn't move through time. Time moves through God. God doesn't move through space, space moves through Him. This is the virtue and consequence of true omnipresence. All places, all times, all dimensions; everywhere there is a where, when, and how simultaneously.

He doesn't present one version of Himself to one group of people and another version to a different group of people. But the funny thing about people is that while God Himself doesn't change, they do. People are constantly in flux, never the exact same person from one minute to the next. With every new experience, change occurs.

With every new thought, new idea, or new choice the person dies and is reborn; remembering everything, or much of everything, that happened before but with a new, or at least altered, understanding of how to interpret it, no matter how small the change may be.

So, God Himself doesn't change, but people do; and different people interpret their experiences of life, other people, and God differently depending on their perception. Some people perceive God as harsh and judgmental; others perceive Him as gentle and loving. God Himself remains motionless.

God Himself remains motionless, but we project motion onto Him. We perceive motion in Him because we ourselves are moving. Just as we perceive motion in the Sun when it rises and sets, but in reality it is the earth that is (and consequently ourselves who are) in motion around the Sun, which, relative to us, remains stationery.

So, God remains stationary, but we perceive Him in motion. We project our own expectations, good or bad, fair or unfair, onto Him. We project our figures of authority, figures of abuse, father figures, mother figures, friendly and enemy figures onto Him depending on what is in the forefront of our minds, or buried deep in our subconscious. We get angry when He doesn't act on what we want, but then ignore Him when He permits events to give us what we need. And, more often than we want to admit, we curse Him for it.

In our life we often project our idea of what He is supposed to be onto Him, and rarely bother to slow down enough to know Him as He is. Often, as with other people, we don't really care about who He is and what He is like, we only care about what we think about Him and what our perception of Him is. We do this often without thinking just because it is how we interact with everybody. Often our perception of a person is formed by who they appeared to be in the past, and has little to do with who they actually are right now, which is always going to be at least slightly different from who they were five minutes ago.

Our biggest problem when knowing God is that He doesn't change, but we do. Our perceptions of Him change and so we perceive that He is changing, when in fact it is we who are changing through the motion and experience of life. So one day we may perceive Him as judgmental and harsh, and another we perceive Him as loving and kind. He has not changed, but our understanding and perception of Him has.

The first rule of getting to know someone is to not form any preconceptions, or to lose one's preconceptions, and then to go and spend time with them and learn *from them* who they are. This applies also to God. We move through time. This is how we experience everything. Things grow old, we grow old, and things change with the passage of time. As we move through time, we encounter Him through every point in time in His stillness. We perceive His absolute stillness as motion because we are in motion even though He is not. Therefore, in order to truly know Him, as He is, we ourselves must slow down and be still as He is still. As we move through Him He reveals Himself, if only we will slow down and pay attention.

God is love in everything He is and does, but we will only experience this if we drop our own perceptions, be still, and get to know Him. He is not harsh and judgmental one minute and kind and loving the next, we are. He does not wish some saved and some damned, we do. He does not send some to heaven and some to hell. We ourselves dwell in either place right now by our own choices, and only through our motion through Him, responding to His Grace, do we move from hell to heaven here and now, and later on.

Jesus said (literally in Greek), "The one who saves his psyche will destroy it, the one who destroys his psyche for My sake will save it." In order to know God, which is our salvation here and now, we must put aside our own projections, perceptions, thoughts, and ideas and just spend time with Him on His terms. Otherwise we attempt to worship only those same ideas, thoughts, and perceptions of what He is like, and not He Himself. This is little different from the idolatry that was so condemned by Him in the Old Testament. He doesn't want us to speculate about Him, He wants us to know Him. He doesn't want us bowing down to a concept we have of Him, He wants us to spend time with Him as He truly is. Idols don't have to be made of wood or stone; they are far more often made of feelings, images, and memories amalgamated together into something that we call God and either love or fear, revere or mock. But such idols are still not Him, and like the Israelites in the Old Testament, He commands that they be torn down so we can know Him as He is.

God remains stationary as we move through Him. Are we paying attention to where we are along the way?

4 | A Ramble about Meditating

My Bishop recently asked me this insightful question, "Do you meditate *in* the presence of God, or do you meditate *to be* in the presence of God? The first is of the heart, the second is of the self." This has been on my mind ever since reading it.

The truth is that when I began my attempts at meditation, it was to experience the presence of God for myself in a controlled setting. Something I could replicate again and again. Without thinking about it, I was basically conducting experiments on God like a lab rat. There really isn't any wonder as to why it became harder and harder after a while, and why He seemed so distant.

God surrounds and fills me. He is the foundation of all existence, and there isn't anywhere I can go where He isn't present. I know that in my head. But it was my perception of His presence, or lack thereof, which was driving my "experimentation."

God surrounds me and I experience Him all the time without recognizing Him for who He is. This is a problem of my own perception, not a lack of His presence. It is a lack of my own awareness and mindfulness (or watchfulness as in the Orthodox tradition). It is therefore possible to experience His presence both in the prayer room and driving our van. Both when saying Mass and when doing the dishes. There are some actions that help one to focus on His presence, but they do not control His presence.

I know that He is in everything. The hard part isn't knowing this. The hard part is the realization of it.

5 | A Ramble about Violating God

H ave you ever felt violated? Imagine someone going through your stuff without permission, or taking compromising photos of you without you knowing about it until it was too late or . . . worse. Have you ever violated someone else, whether you meant to or not?

This might take some explanation, but follow my train of thought with me.

The creation, including ourselves, is to God as sound is to air, or wave is to water. The energy that makes up all matter and energy in the universe is ultimately derived from His Existence, and used to form the waves, particles, and dimensions that make up existence as we know it. Everything is not God, but God is in everything. He is the foundation of all Creation, and maintains it by His will alone.

The consequence of this is that He knows every particle, every bit of energy that makes up you or me. He is intimately involved with it. He knows everything you or I know. He feels everything you or I feel. He experiences everything you or I experience.

What then must it seem like to Him when we act selfishly? When I do something to please myself at the expense of someone else (which is always the case when acting selfishly, someone else always pays a price)? What must it seem like when we hold a grudge, steal, or hurt someone in any way, shape, or form?

I remember in Bible School one of my professors quoting a verse from Psalm 51, "Against You, and You only have I sinned." David wrote this Psalm after he had gotten Bathsheba pregnant and had her husband killed. My professor then went on to say that all sin is ultimately an offense against God and no one else.

A lot of people get hurt when we act selfishly. A lot of people are affected; often many that we don't know because of the ripple effect it has. But ultimately, when we are selfish or self-centered, the Person we are violating most is God Himself.

Part V | Grace, Salvation, and Other Theological Subjects

1 | A Letter to A Pastor about the Common Anchors of Our Faith

Brother Pastor,

I've been doing a lot of thinking about how we might all work together towards a common goal without our conflicting theologies muddying the issues at hand.

The first thing is that we all share the same goal: to guide both ourselves and our respective flocks in moving from our initial profession of faith or conversion experience, "Point A", to the final point of our salvation, which we'll call "point B." We call "point B" by different terms, depending on which tradition or theology one belongs to. In Evangelical Protestant circles it's called Glorification (one

of the three "tenses" of salvation: justification, sanctification, and glorification). In Catholic and Orthodox circles it's called variously "beatification, divinization, or deification," and theologically

"theosis." As I understand the term, it's where we come into full union with God, both losing and maintaining the distinction between Him and ourselves. Various Protestant denominations define it with slight variations or understandings, but it basically works out to the same effect. So, our purpose is to move, or be moved, from point A to point B, and to help guide others along that same Path. With that in mind, we have to be especially careful that we ourselves walk the Path, know what it is, what it looks like, and how to get to the destination point.

I noticed a long time ago, when I first became Catholic, that the life of a Christian who is sincere in their faith looks pretty much the same from denomination to denomination. That is, while theologies and interpretations differ, we all tend to be moved either internally or externally towards several guideposts along the way.

The first one the newly converted or professed moves towards is Baptism. I know we all tend to disagree on the nature and necessity of Baptism, but in general we all usually agree that someone who has had a real conversion to Jesus Christ will generally at least want to follow Him in Baptism. Further, He told us to do it. We all accept that there are some circumstances where it simply isn't possible (immediate martyrdom, thief on the cross, etc.), and we have our own theological explanations around it. But in general, it's the normal course of action, and it can be reasonably assumed that there is a spiritual problem with the professed person who refuses to commit to Christ in Baptism.

The next one that the Christian moves towards is Holy Communion, or Holy Eucharist. Again, we all tend to disagree on the meaning and necessity of Holy Eucharist. But again, it is something He told us to do, at the very least, to remember His death until He comes. Like Baptism, it has been a part of the tradition and practice of the universal Church, however it's practiced, since the Apostles. Again, we consider something to generally be spiritually wrong with the Christian who either refuses Holy Eucharist or treats it in a profane or dishonorable way.

Of course when we sin, knowingly or unknowingly, we are convicted and moved towards repentance and confession, either directly to God or with a member of the clergy. Often, even in Protestant circles, a person who feels particularly convicted about a sin will seek out a Pastor for counsel and to help guide them back. That is a part of our responsibility as guides and shepherds, assistant or otherwise, whether or not one accepts the Apostolic authority to bind and loose.

In the process of this, we also all generally seek out other Christians to fellowship with. And, depending on the denomination, we can seek official adult church membership, Baptism of the Holy Spirit, or (in the Catholic/Orthodox faith) Confirmation, especially if the profession of faith was made for us by our parents at a very young age.

If we get sick, we tend to go to the leadership of the Church and ask them to pray for our healing. Depending on the denomination, oil tends to be involved. We generally call this the Anointing of the Sick, and whether viewed as a Sacrament or not, I haven't seen a church yet that doesn't practice it.

The call to get married and the call to Ordination, or both, are also practiced in virtually every Church, although not by everyone because not everyone is called to either or both. Ordination is generally practiced exclusively by the laying-on of hands by virtually every denomination, as it has been for two thousand years.

So, these are the first guideposts along the way. In the Catholic/ Orthodox tradition, they are the seven Sacraments, and they tend to be represented, recognized as such or not, in Christian practice regardless of denomination.

We generally tend to recognize, also, that there is something spiritually wrong with the Christian, baptized or otherwise, who after knowingly sinning, refuses to turn away from that sin, or admit any wrongdoing. We have all watched as that professed Christian, if he doesn't repent, goes into a downward spiral and his visible spiritual state gets worse and worse until he descends into a kind of living hell of his own. We all have different explanations theologically as to why and how. But the observable phenomenon is the same, and we instinctively mourn the loss of the brother or sister, whether or not we accept that their salvation is still secured.

Further, we can all generally agree, willingly or begrudgingly, that to walk the Path of Jesus Christ as He taught it requires some will and visible effort on our part, and that the visible indication of one who is on that Path is love, compassion, and kindness for the brothers, for the stranger, for those who hate us, and especially for God Himself. The one who follows Jesus Christ offers himself or herself as a living sacrifice just as He did. And the pretender tends to be pretty easy to spot, whether or not he or she realizes it at the moment.

Our observable goal is union with God, both in this life as well as the next, and our movement must always be towards this. Another thing that I think we can all generally agree on, if we really think about it, is that this doesn't come without the cross. It doesn't come without accepting that there is a fundamental malfunction in the human psyche (and I would argue the continuous recognition of this by the Christian as well as the convert), and that union with Jesus Christ in His death on the Cross is the only solution. As we surrender to that union in His death, so also His resurrection and the life of God will become more apparent in us until nothing else remains of us except the distinction between "He and I." In this, we realize and experience what is truly the absolute center of His infinite Being: an all-consuming, devastating, and blissful love.

These are just some thoughts on truths I think we can all use as anchors to achieve the same ends and avoid unnecessary and useless bickering which only serves to make us look like morons who don't understand the truth ourselves, and drive people away from Christ. And if we can all build on these anchors to direct and guide the people, in this case especially the youth because they are at a point now where they can absorb truth like a new wineskin absorbing new wine, then we can truly fulfill the command of Christ to go and make disciples.

If you think this is a positive step in the right direction, share these thoughts with the other pastors and see what they think and let me know.

In Christ,

Fr. Allen+

2 | A Ramble About "Once Saved, Always Saved"

Let me be clear on this subject. Nowhere in this ramble do I ever express the belief that someone can "accidentally" lose their salvation. I also do not say, under any circumstances, that anyone can earn their salvation. With this in mind, let's continue.

I don't make any secret about what I think of this particular Reformation doctrine. I have seen more damage done both to individual Christian lives and the Church as a whole through this particular teaching than almost any other doctrine. All too many people, because of this doctrine, seem to believe and live as though because they said a prayer or made a public profession of faith they can live their lives however they want and they will be fine because they have "fire insurance." This is far removed from the teachings of the ancient Church, and was never even considered until the sixteenth century. I take my stand on this teaching directly from both Holy Scripture and the unbroken orthodox teaching of the Church as it has stood since the Apostles.

This teaching is also known as the "Perseverance of the Saints," and was initially introduced in modern times during the Reformation.

In particular, it was promoted by John Calvin and later became an integral part of the Calvinist theology. Today, put in layman's terms, it simply teaches that all those who have truly put their faith in Christ, "accepted Christ," can never lose their salvation regardless of what they do or say. They are locked into it.

On the surface this sounds great, and it is often promoted as a great comfort. And it does sound very comforting. The problem with this teaching is that it runs contradictory to a number of passages of Sacred Scripture, while professing to uphold a number of others, essentially pitting Scripture against Scripture. Furthermore, it requires that the teaching of the Church on salvation since ancient times be thrown out entirely and viewed as somehow heretical. The teaching itself is comparatively very recent (within the last five hundred years), and proponents of it presume that those Saints who lived prior to it either weren't "saved," or that the salvific mechanism was in place regardless of their understanding of it. The presumption is made that somehow the Gospel was either taught incompletely, or not fully received, until the Reformation. Consider what that presumption is saying for just a moment. At the very least, it means that the Apostles and those who immediately followed them didn't understand the Gospel in its entirety.

Another problem arises in the practical application of this teaching. All too often, the state of one's eternal salvation is considered settled once they make some kind of public, or even private, profession of faith in Christ. Many times one is asked to "pray the prayer," or is led in some kind of a prayer. Once the person has accomplished this, they are considered "saved" and the "evangelist" moves on to the next lost soul assuming that nothing else needs to be done with the new convert. They are "saved" and so they have everything they need. All too often the person who was "saved" falls back into the same pattern of life they were in. Ironically, if the behavior becomes too immoral, the person's salvation is then questioned as though their acceptance of Christ somehow didn't "take."

In dealing with this topic I know I'm going to have to be very careful because of the tangled mess this teaching has caused, and because of the number of issues involved and the number of issues it confuses. For example, the "faith versus works" controversy often arises in discussing this issue. Also, the issue arises as to whether or not we could ever do something that God couldn't or wouldn't forgive. Also, some bring up the argument as to whether or not we could ever lose God's love, as though this might play into it. Always Holy Scripture is used to justify each and every position, contradictory or not. Always the ancient teaching of the Church, and it's interpretation of Holy Scripture, is ignored and treated as somehow heretical regardless of (or perhaps because of) its antiquity.

So, let's touch briefly on what the ancient Church had to say about this issue from those documents and writers accepted by the Church as Orthodox (meaning "right teaching"):

"We ought therefore, brethren, carefully to inquire concerning our salvation. Otherwise, the wicked one, having made his entrance by deceit, may hurl us forth from our life." (The Epistle of Barnabas written between 70 and 130 AD.)

"Let us therefore repent with the whole heart, so that none of us perish by the way . . . Let us then practice righteousness so that we may be saved unto the end." (Second Clement, written around 150 AD)

"Those who do not obey Him, being disinherited by Him, have ceased to be His sons." (Irenaeus, Bishop of Lyons, around 180 AD)

"It is neither the faith, nor the love, nor the hope, nor the endurance of one day; rather, 'he that endures to the end will be saved.'" (Clement of Alexandria, writing around 195 AD)

"No one is a Christian but he who perseveres to the end." (Tertullian, Presbyter at Carthage, writing around 197 AD)

"You are still in the world. You are still in the battlefield. You daily fight for your lives. So you must be careful that . . . what you have begun to be with such a blessed commencement will be consummated in you. It is a small thing to have first received something. It is a greater thing to be able to keep what you have attained. Faith itself and the saving birth do not make alive by merely being received. Rather, they must be preserved. It is not the actual attainment, but the perfecting, that keeps a man for God. The Lord taught this in His instruction when He said, 'Look! You have been made whole. Sin no more, lest a worse thing come upon you.'. . . Solomon, Saul, and many others were able to keep the grace given to them so long as they walked in the Lord's ways. However, when the discipline of the Lord was forsaken by them, grace also forsook them." (Cyprian, Bishop of Carthage, written around 250 AD)

"As to one who again denies Christ, no special previous standing can be effective to him for salvation. For anyone of us will hold it necessary that whatever is the last thing to be found in a man in this respect, that is where he will be judged. All of those things that he has previously done are wiped away and obliterated." (Cyprian's Treatise on Re-Baptism, written around 257 AD)

"True repentance makes a man cautious and diligent to avoid the faults into which he has once fallen through treachery. No one can be so prudent and so cautious as not at some time to slip. Therefore, God, knowing our weakness, out of His compassion has opened a harbor of refuge for man--that the medicine of repentance might aid this necessity to which our frailty is liable." (Lactantius, Christian tutor writing between 304 and 313 AD)

I could go on, but then this would become a book rather than just a Ramble. The teaching and understanding of the Church, even prior to the first Council of Nicea in 325 AD was quite clear, and also followed after what Jesus Himself actually said in the Gospels. In short, if, after a person has accepted Christ and been baptized, he continues in his sin and does not repent, he will not be saved. The teaching of the Church is also clear that struggling with one's sin, and making mistakes, and backsliding, and even kicking and screaming are understood to be a part of the process of spiritual maturity. The key here is repentance and confession: turning away from the things you've done wrong and turning to God.

In short, our salvation requires our cooperation. The state in which we end is far more important than the state in which we begin our faith in Christ. Ezekiel 18:21-30 says:

"But if a wicked person turns away from all his sins that he has committed and keeps all my statutes and does what is just and right, he shall surely live; he shall not die. None of the transgressions that he has committed shall be remembered against him; for the righteousness that he has done he shall live. Have I any pleasure in the death of the wicked, declares the Lord GOD, and not rather that he should turn from his way and live? But when a righteous person turns away from his righteousness and does injustice and does the same abominations that the wicked person does, shall he live? None of the righteous deeds that he has done shall be remembered; for the treachery of which he is guilty and the sin he has committed, for them he shall die. Yet you say, 'The way of the Lord is not just.' Hear now, O house of Israel: Is my way not just? Is it not your ways that are not just? When a righteous person turns away from his righteousness and does injustice, he shall die for it; for the injustice that he has done he shall die.

"Again, when a wicked person turns away from the wickedness he has committed and does what is just and right, he shall save his life. Because he considered and turned away from all the transgressions that he had committed, he shall surely live; he shall not die. Yet the house of Israel says, 'The way of the Lord is not just.' O house of Israel, are my ways not just? Is it not your ways that are not just? Therefore I will judge you, O house of Israel, every one according to his ways, declares the Lord GOD. Repent and turn from all your transgressions, lest iniquity be your ruin." (ESV)

Another passage to consider is John 15:4-6,

"Abide in me, and I in you. As the branch cannot bear fruit by itself, unless it abides in the vine, neither can you, unless you abide in me. I am the vine; you are the branches. Whoever abides in me and I in him, he it is that bears much fruit, for apart from me you can do nothing. If anyone does not abide in me he is thrown away like a branch and withers; and the branches are gathered, thrown into the fire, and burned." (ESV)

Also, 1 John 1:5-10,

"This is the message we have heard from him and proclaim to you, that God is light, and in him is no darkness at all. If we say we have fellowship with him while we walk in darkness, we lie and do not practice the truth. But if we walk in the light, as he is in the light, we have fellowship with one another, and the blood of Jesus his Son cleanses us from all sin. If we say we have no sin, we deceive ourselves, and the truth is not in us. If we confess our sins, he is faithful and just to forgive us our sins and to cleanse us from all unrighteousness. If we say we have not sinned, we make him a liar, and his word is not in us." (ESV)

Where then, if it is possible to fall away, is our hope, our assurance, and our comfort? How could anyone feel secure knowing that it was possible to fail? Let me ask this question: Why would anyone bother to make progress in their faith and discipleship if it *wasn't* possible to fail?

But here is our hope in Jesus Christ that, if we fall, He will raise us back up. If we sin, He will forgive. But here is also our warning, that if we treat His blood as nothing, take it for granted, and do not repent of it, He will not open the door for us. He will ask who we are and send us away violently. God is not stupid (as all too often we treat Him). He knows who His friends are, and who they aren't. He knows with whom He has a solid relationship and who only pay Him lip service. He knows those who love Him but are visibly struggling, and those who couldn't care less about Him but appear to have it all together.

Those who profess faith in Christ and then deny Him by their actions will also be denied by Him, because, contrary to popular theology, faith and actions are not opposing forces. They are one and the same. Faith is action, and action is faith. You will never act on a belief you do not possess. In the same way, you will never fail to act on a belief you do possess. Whether what you say you believe and what you actually believe are the same thing is another matter entirely, and requires deep introspection and complete honesty with yourself and with God, who is more than willing and capable of helping you in this regard. Often we want to see ourselves as believing something, when in fact we believe something quite contrary to what we want to believe we believe. (This is, I think, another aspect of the Disorder to which we are all subject, that we do not want to be totally honest with ourselves because it could reveal some flaw within us that we do not wish to see, but I digress . . .)

Our final salvation is not locked down until the day we finally shed this body. Until then, we will fight. We will win some battles against ourselves, and lose others. And always God has His hand outstretched to us, calling us to learn from those mistakes and failures and return to Him, where He can and will lift us up. If we cry out, "God have mercy on me, a sinner!" He will hear us, even if it is with our dying breath. If we walk away from Him never to return, even if no one else knows it, He hears those silent footsteps too, and mourns.

3 | A Ramble about the Force

"The Force?"

"The Force is an energy field produced by all living things. It binds us, and penetrates us, and holds the galaxy together." . .

"You mean it controls your actions?"

"Partially, but it also obeys your commands."

(From the dialogue in *Star Wars Episode IV: A New Hope* between Obi-Wan Kenobi and Luke Skywalker)

We have to use a lot of analogies in describing spiritual realities. Some analogies are better than others. Some analogies come closer to the truth than others. And where someone may understand the truth trying to be conveyed by one analogy, the same analogy may be unintelligible to the next person.

Grace is one such concept that is difficult to explain. It is made even more difficult because of the theological confusion that has been introduced by some Reformation theology. As a backlash against the Catholic Church, rather than relying on the teaching of the Church prior to the Reformation, a much different, weakened understanding of it based on the literal meaning of the Greek word has rendered it to mean little more than God's favor or good will towards man.

(This is largely due to the sincere, but misguided dogma of the Reformation known as "Sola Scriptura" or "Scripture Only.")

In the teaching of the Church, Grace means far more than this, but explaining it, and how it operates, isn't the easiest of things. When explained in the wrong way it sounds like you're trying to earn or merit it based on your own good works, and thus trying to earn your own salvation, which is impossible.

As simply put as possible, the Fathers of the Church describe Grace as a part of the "uncreated energies of God," and the "presence of God outside of His persons." St. Maximos describes these energies as "eternally existent, proceeding from the eternally existing God." St. Gregory Palamas writes "Thus God possesses both essence and that which is not essence, even if it should not be called an accident, namely, the divine will and energy." The essence of God is that which is totally "other," unknowable, and unapproachable, whereas the energies of God are close at hand, within our experience, and approachable. (Quotations from *The Philokalia, vols. II & IV*)

The final goal of the Christian life is deification (in Greek, "theosis", sometimes called "divinization," in Protestant Evangelical circles called "glorification"), the total union with God, and full participation in His nature outside of His essence. The Fathers say to this effect, "God became man so that man might become god." St. Irenaeus writes, "Our Lord Jesus Christ, through His transcendent love, became what we are, so that He might bring us to be even what He Himself is." The illustration often used by the Fathers is that of a piece of metal, when it is put into a fire, takes on the properties of the fire, the heat and the light, even glowing much like the fire, while still retaining it's identity as metal. Grace is the energy of God that accomplishes deification.

That's the beginning of the explanation. The next part of it is where we run into all kinds of trouble, accusations, and theological ruts. That's because, while Grace is freely given by God, it doesn't generally come while we are just doing our own thing. Grace in some respects is like electricity, in that you must be plugged in for it to flow.

Jesus essentially spelled it out in John 15:4-7. He said, "Remain in me, and I in you . . . without me you can do nothing . . . if anyone doesn't remain in me he is cast out as a branch, withers, and is thrown into the fire . . . if you remain in me and my word remains in you, you will ask what you desire and it shall be done for you." So, in order for Grace to flow, you have to be plugged into Jesus. If you're unplugged, and stay unplugged through your own choices, not only will Grace not flow, but you get tossed out like a bunch of dead branches. But, if you're plugged in and stay plugged in, remembering what He taught and said, anything is possible for you.

So, how do we stay plugged in? The short answer is obedience to what Jesus taught, prayer (discursive and contemplative), and participation in the Sacraments, especially Baptism and Holy Eucharist. It's not a matter of earning or meriting Grace, but staying plugged in. And as we adhere to these things in humility, self-control, and renunciation of attachments, Grace, the uncreated energy of God, flows through us and allows us to progress even further in prayer, obedience, and the Sacraments in a self-perpetuating cycle. This cycle is only broken as we leave off and go our own way. In other words, the only way Grace won't flow is if we willingly unplug from Jesus and ignore it.

What are commonly called the "Spiritual Gifts" are also powered by Grace. The closer you draw to Jesus, the longer you remain consistently plugged in, the more evident they become. This is born out even by the Greek word for them, "charismata," which could be translated "grace abilities." Without Grace, they simply won't function, similar to an unplugged lamp. This is why so many Christians rely on their own natural abilities and try to pass off things like teaching ability, public speaking, or natural "charisma" as a spiritual gift. They have no experience with the real thing because, even after baptism, they choose to pursue their own things and remain unplugged from Jesus, often not being taught otherwise by their respective local churches. You can't walk in the Spirit if you're indulging in the flesh (sensual desires, avarice, self-esteem, etc.). The two are opposed to each other and if one is in control, the other can't be (see Galatians 5:16-23).

This leads us back to my quotation from Star Wars at the beginning of this ramble. A good analogy I have found for Grace is "the Force" (yes, it sounds at best creepy, but hear me out). The Force is the source of a Jedi's power and abilities, and without it he is unable to do anything, much like Grace to the Christian. The impossible jumps, the pulling x-wings out of swamps, the holding boulders high above the head by a teeny tiny green Jedi Master; all of these are impossible without the Jedi being plugged into the Force. In the same way, the replication of the life, power, and person of Jesus Christ within the Christian, in other words the process of "deification," is impossible without being plugged into Him, with His Grace flowing through that person as a result. Like the Force as well, we must cooperate with Grace. God will not force us to do anything that we will not agree to, any more than the Force will force a Jedi to jump twenty feet in the air without his permission. The Grace of God binds us, penetrates us, and holds everything together.

Our salvation is accomplished truly by Grace, through Faith. It is the gift of God so that no one can brag that he earned it. Salvation is impossible without the Grace of God, and is energized and effected by it. Holy Scripture is clear about this. But Holy Scripture is equally clear that just saying you have faith is not enough. You must act on that faith, or else it isn't true faith but is mere words, and words alone are meaningless without the actions to back them up. Grace won't flow until faith itself is realized by action.

4 | A Ramble about The Expensive Pearl

In one of His parables, Jesus said that the Kingdom of Heaven was like a very expensive pearl or treasure hidden in a field, which when a person finds it, he goes and sells everything he has to buy that field. In other words, gaining the Kingdom of Heaven is worth giving up and letting go of everything else as though it were worthless in comparison.

So the question then becomes, what about the Kingdom of Heaven is so worth it? Whether we like to admit it or not, this is a question which we ask ourselves. And I know this is a serious question, a question of doubt, which we ask ourselves by how we act and the choices we make in what we pursue. What is the expensive treasure that Jesus said would be so worth it? In other words, why should we do what Jesus said? Why bother renouncing everything? Why bother denying yourself? Why not just fake it? Just sit in the pew on Sundays and put on a "good Christian facade?" It's a heck of a lot easier to try and stay out of the line of fire in both directions than the alternatives.

We need to understand what's at stake. We already know about the one direction, backwards. We know what awaits us there, and it is terrifying. But what about forwards? What goal awaits us on the other end of the trials, the poverty, the humiliation, the self-control, the picking up one's cross in humble obedience? What is the final goal of all of this?

God Himself.

The entire goal of salvation is what is called in Greek, "theosis," and in English "deification." Put simply, it is a human being taking on the nature of God, sharing His life fully and completely in everything except His Essence or Substance. The Fathers of the Church wrote about it in explicit terms which would make a lot of Christians do a double take, and perhaps even have heart attacks, at the language used (citations are taken from Bercot's *Dictionary of Early Christian Beliefs* and the *Wikipedia.org* article on "divinization"):

St. Irenaeus of Lyons: "Our Lord Jesus Christ, through His transcendent love, became what we are in order to make us what he is himself."

St. Clement of Alexandria: "He who obeys the Lord and follows the prophecy given through him . . . becomes a god while still moving about in the flesh."

St. Athanasius: "God became man so that men might become gods."

St. Cyril of Alexandria: "[We] are called 'temples of God' and indeed 'gods', and so we are."

St. Gregory of Nazianzus: " . . . become gods for God's sake, since (God) became man for our sake."

St. Augustine: "God was made man, that man might be made God." . . . "It is clear that he called men gods being deified by his grace and not born of his substance. For he justified, who is just of himself and not from another, and he deifies, who is god of himself and not by participation in another. . . . If we have been made sons of God, we have been made gods; but this is by grace of adoption and not of the nature of our begetter." . . . "Our full adoption as sons will take place in the redemption of our body. We now have the first fruits of the spirit, by which we are indeed made sons of God. In other respects, however, since we are not yet finally saved, we are therefore not yet fully made new, not yet sons of God but children of the world."

St. John of the Cross: "In thus allowing God to work in it, the soul . . . is at once illumined and transformed in God, and God communicates to it His supernatural Being, in such wise that it appears to be God Himself, and has all that God Himself has. And this union comes to pass when God grants the soul this supernatural favour, that all the things of God and the soul are one in participant transformation; and the soul seems to be God rather than a soul, and is indeed God by participation; although it is true that its natural being, though thus transformed, is as distinct from the Being of God as it was before."

Orthodox Bishop Kallistos (Timothy) Ware writes, "By virtue of this distinction between the divine essence and the divine energies, we are able to affirm the possibility of a direct or mystical union between man and God—what the Greek Fathers term the 'theosis' of man, his 'deification'--but at the same time we exclude any pantheistic identification between the two: for man participates in the energies of God, not in the essence. There is union, but not fusion or confusion. Although 'oned' with the divine, man still remains man; he is not swallowed up or annihilated, but between him and God there continues always to exist an 'I—Thou' relationship of person to person." (*The Orthodox Way*, Kallistos Ware)

You must forgive the Church Fathers for using the admittedly disturbing word "gods" because there was simply no other good word available to them to describe it. How do you describe this kind of thing accurately no matter what language you use? This is what it means to be sons of God, having received the full Adoption through Christ Jesus, bodies included, in the Resurrection.

Deification is the goal of salvation. It is the end result. It doesn't fully happen until after death. But one thing that must be made clear: this is a teaching of the Church, has been since the beginning, and still is today. In other denominations and Christian theologies it is called "glorification," and it is also referred to as "divinization."

The Fathers that I quoted were not some fringe group of radicals; they were the pillars and foundations of the Ancient Church. For example, St. Athanasius was the principle advocate for the doctrine of the Holy Trinity as we know it at the Ecumenical Councils, which laid out and defined what we know as the Nicene Creed, the standard of faith of the Church. St. Irenaeus was the Bishop of Lyons and an important theologian and apologist of the second century. St. Augustine of Hippo should need no explanation as the author of *The City of God*, and the *Confessions*, neither should St. John of the Cross as the author of *The Dark Night of the Soul.*

The Holy Scriptures themselves refer to it several times:

John 10:34-36 (ESV)

Jesus answered them, "Is it not written in your Law, 'I said, you are gods'? If he called them gods to whom the word of God came—and Scripture cannot be broken—do you say of him whom the Father consecrated and sent into the world, 'You are blaspheming,' because I said, 'I am the Son of God?'"

John 17:20-23 (ESV)

"I do not ask for these only, but also for those who will believe in me through their word, that they may all be one, just as you, Father, are in me, and I in you, that they also may be in us, so that the world may believe that you have sent me. The glory that you have given me I have given to them, that they may be one even as we are one, I in them and you in me, that they may become perfectly one, so that the world may know that you sent me and loved them even as you loved me."

Hebrews 3:14 (ESV)

"For we have become partakers of Christ, if truly we hold the beginning of the assurance firm to the end; . . . "

2 Peter 1:3-4 (ESV)

"As His divine power has given to us all things pertaining to life and godliness through the full knowledge of the One calling us through glory and virtue, by which means He has given to us the very great and precious promises, so that through these you might be partakers of the divine nature, escaping from the corruption in the world by lust."

1 John 3:2-3 (ESV)

"Beloved, now we are the children of God, and it was not yet revealed what we shall be. But we know that if He is revealed, we shall be like Him, because we shall see Him as He is. And everyone having this hope on Him purifies himself even as that *One* is pure."

The purpose of the Cross was for us to enter into union with God through our union with Christ in baptism (see Romans 6). This is the beginning of our union with Him, but it is by no means the end or culmination. The process of sanctification is to further that realization of union achieved largely through prayer, Sacraments, and obedience, as I have discussed previously. But the culmination of that union is full theosis, where we take on the full nature of God without losing the distinction between us.

The Fathers agreed that full deification couldn't be achieved in this life until after the death of the body, but by Grace the goal and purpose of our discipleship is to progress towards full deification in this life. In this, there is no middle ground. Either we progress towards this kind of "ascension," or we regress into our sin disorder and eternal darkness. There is no "safe" place where we can just remain static for fear of the cross, or fear of hell. Let me say this again just to be clear, you either progress on the path of Jesus Christ towards deification, or you fall backwards. There is no way to stand still.

It is the teaching of Holy Scripture that we are united to Christ Jesus through baptism into His death. Deification begins, but does not reach it's fulfillment, here. As we engage in the "cycle of Grace," His Grace, His uncreated energy, becomes more and more active in our lives, transforming us as we partake or share in His nature through Christ. The end result is that we become divinity without becoming The Divine. We take on the nature of Deity while remaining human. We are in full union with Him while remaining separate beings from Him.

The promise of what we will be through our union with Jesus Christ is something mind-boggling and hard to wrap the head around. It is achieved only through cooperation with the Grace of God, letting go of those things that are behind, and reaching forward to what is in front of us. As St. Paul said, "But whatever gain I had, I counted as loss for the sake of Christ. Indeed, I count everything as loss because of the surpassing worth of knowing Christ Jesus my Lord. For his sake I have suffered the loss of all things and count them as rubbish, in order that I may gain Christ and be found in him, not having a righteousness of my own that comes from the law, but that which comes through faith in Christ, the righteousness from God that depends on faith—that I may know him and the power of his resurrection, and may share his sufferings, becoming like him in his death, that by any means possible I may attain the resurrection from the dead. Not that I have already obtained this or am already perfect, but I press on to make it my own, because Christ Jesus has made me his own. Brothers, I do not consider that I have made it my own. But one thing I do: forgetting what lies behind and straining forward to what lies ahead, I press on toward the goal for the prize of the upward call of God in Christ Jesus." (Philippians 3:7-14, ESV)

St. Paul believed this was worth considering everything else in his life, everything that was considered an advantage to him, to be rubbish. He wanted this and was willing to throw away everything else to get it. This is the high calling of God in Christ Jesus, and it really can't get much higher. The Church Fathers called it as they saw it.

This is to what we, like St. Paul, are called. This is the goal, and it isn't just handed to us on a silver platter as a certain popular teaching professes. St. Paul knew that He hadn't attained to it yet, and wouldn't attain to it in this life, but what does he say?

"Not that I have already obtained this or am already perfect, but I press on to make it my own, because Christ Jesus has made me his own. Brothers, I do not consider that I have made it my own. But one thing I do: forgetting what lies behind and straining forward to what lies ahead, I press on toward the goal for the prize of the upward call of God in Christ Jesus."(Philippians 3:12-14, ESV)

He continued on, shedding everything that could possibly hold him back from reaching it, even in this life, and encouraged and taught others to do the same. He held it up in front of them and basically said, "Here it is! This is the finish line! Keep your sights set on this and dump everything which could hamper you getting there!" When you're running a race to win, you don't carry a bunch of extra weight with you, and you don't stop in the middle of the race and call it good. We are called to seek full deification in this life, or at least get as close as possible to it. This is the process of sanctification.

I have said this before, Eternal Life begins here and now, not when you stop breathing. Deification is Eternal Life. It is the Kingdom of Heaven and it is worth everything to attain it in the here and now.

We are disturbed by the use of such phrases as, "God became man so that men might become gods." It isn't language that we use today in this world. It sounds heretical, like something from the Latter Day Saints, or something out of the New Age movement. These are only perversions of what it really means. It really means shedding this corruptible body for an incorruptible. It means shedding this mortality for what is immortal. It means receiving our adoption as sons of God in full. And it does not come from giving up the race in the middle.

So, I ask you, is this worth it? Would the prospect of inherited deity be enough to renounce everything and follow Jesus Christ? In the garden, the serpent promised that Adam and Eve would be like God if they ate the fruit of the tree, because they would know good from evil. What they got was a hereditary insanity that we all share which makes us all think we know better than God or anyone else. What God promises us through the Gospel of Jesus Christ is nothing short of being made like Him in every way but His Essence or Being.

Theosis is Eternal Life. It is the Kingdom of Heaven. It is the treasure waiting on the other side of the pain and loss. Is that worth it to you?

5 | A Ramble about Law vs. Grace

Okay, so here's the issue, Law vs. Grace – or is it? St. Paul says in Galatians that the law was our schoolmaster to bring us to Christ. Literally, our "pedagogue." And once Christ appeared there was no more need for the Law.

First of all, let's define what was meant by "Law." The Jewish people of the period would have understood this word as "Torah," the legal code, or "constitution" if you will, for the people of Israel. It was, principally, a Suzerainty treaty between Israel and her Sovereign King, Yahweh her God. It was a code of conduct that separated Israel from the other nations around her. The terms were pretty easy to understand as much as any constitution or penal code would be. "If you do this (fill in the blank), then this is the consequence."

Contrary to popular opinion, penal codes in general are amoral, as are constitutions. They are also simply agreements between the government and the people, and the terms of that agreement may be either beneficial (hopefully) or harmful to the people who are governed by them. The penal code makes no distinction between good motives or bad motives, it simply says "this is the regulation, and these are the consequences."

It's important to make this distinction, that the law, the Torah, was and is amoral; neither good nor evil as such (although no one would argue that the legal code described in the Torah is somehow bad, or not inherently good or beneficial), in the same way that penal codes and constitutions are neither good nor evil as such. They simply are what they are.

The human psyche since the fall latches on to ideas, concepts, and actions as either good or evil, right or wrong. It is important to understand that this is a malfunction of the psyche due to ingesting the fruit, and the inherent disobedience that occurred when that happened. This is not, and never has been, a normal or natural function of the human psyche. We weren't created with it, and the "penal code" set down was specifically meant to keep it from happening. "Don't eat the fruit . . . if you do, you will die." The assumption of knowing good from evil by a human being is a direct byproduct and consequence of that action. It is a part of that death which was warned about.

As a result, every human being since is born with this innate psychological need to label thoughts, ideas, concepts, and actions as either good or evil, depending on whether the human being in question agrees with the thought, idea, concept, or action.

The Law, the Torah, was given to regulate this. It was a concession of mercy, as God so often does, taking human beings where they are at, recognizing their weaknesses and saying, "Okay, I'll work with you on this. I know this is all you can handle and is how you think at the moment." So the Torah was given to train human beings, that cannot and have not experienced God from birth, towards compassion, mercy, justice, love, and, most importantly, knowing Him. But because the Torah itself is amoral, the malfunction in the human psyche latches on to it and says "Okay, now I know this is good and that is evil," and it does so without mercy, because mercy is a foreign concept to the malfunction, if not to the psyche as a whole. The Torah worked in conjunction with the malfunction to train the Israeli people as long as they adhered to it, surrendering their perception of "good" and "evil" to the tenets of the Torah. But it didn't work if they didn't relinquish this perception and accept the better judgment of God, who wrote it. And, while it can train a people towards compassion, mercy, and knowing Him, it cannot naturally repair the malfunction that prevents this understanding in the first place.

The issue is not law vs. grace. Because even if you remove the "law" or any legal code as a factor, you will still have that malfunctioning psyche which says "this is right and that is wrong," arbitrarily assigning those values to whatever it does or does not agree with. The repair only comes through union with God through Jesus Christ. But even after the union with Christ through baptism, when the repair has begun, the psyche must still be retrained from its old habit of "good vs. evil," and relating to the world in that way. The scriptures use the analogy of a "new man" and an "old man;" literally a "new human being" and an "old human being," and these two "human beings" are opposed to one another.

Because while God has now grafted or "glued" Himself to you through Christ, the psyche doesn't just automatically understand how to make use of this new state of being. This is new input, if you will, and it will attempt to force the new input through the old method of processing. The new capability must be integrated, independent from the "good vs. evil" malfunction, into the psyche's way of doing things. It must relearn how to interpret the world and relationships around it through the experience of God and union with Him.

So, the discussion is really about judgment vs. love, not law vs. grace. Because law, a code of conduct designed to regulate human behavior and prevent harm in conjunction with the malfunctioning psyche, is irrelevant when love, which realizes the union with God independent of the malfunction, is practiced and active. But judgment, the need to designate this as good and that as evil and enforce it on others, is a malfunction and a result of the greater psychological malfunction of not having the absolute security of being able to experience God from birth as human beings were made to.

6 | A Ramble about Holy Eucharist

If you're like me, you not only have a computer, but sometimes it seems like it's surgically attached to your hand. When I get bored sometimes, I start rearranging the "Desktop" on my computer. I change the themes and icons, and I also rearrange the icons, or "desktop shortcuts," which start the different applications directly from the "Desktop."

I don't really need these icons; or application launchers if you prefer. Most of them sit unused on my screen because I don't use the programs they represent that often. On my wife's old computer screen hordes of these icons just sat, and we had to periodically clean them off. On an average PC, you don't really get a choice as to whether or not they're put there. When you install a program, it parks one or more of these little pictures right on the Desktop so that you can admire them in all their glory.

As annoying as these little icons can be, they actually serve a very handy and useful function for the programs you use most of the time. Remember way back in the day when Dinosaurs ruled the earth and most average cavemen ran some version of what was called DOS on their computers? There was no friendly picture display. You actually had to know where the program itself was located on your computer. If you wanted to run a program called "program.exe," for example, you would likely have to type something like "C:\folder1\ folder2\program.exe" at the command line, or you would have to manually change directories by typing "cd folder1 . . . cd folder2 . . . program." Thankfully programmers became enlightened that not everyone wanted to spend their productive years memorizing DOS commands, and, to strains of the hallelujah chorus, the graphical user interface (GUI) was invented.

These days, a similar approach if you didn't have any shortcuts would be to dig through the file browser. For example, if you had to launch your word processor you'd have to continuously click folders in the file browser, until you reached a file called "swriter.exe." It would look something like C:\ -> Program Files -> OpenOffice.org 3 -> program -> swriter.exe. You would soon be truly annoyed and confused if you had to follow the same procedure for every web browser, word processor, email client, picture viewer, media player, and game that you wanted to run on your computer.

Enter the Desktop shortcut or application launcher. A lot of folks probably think these are the actual programs themselves, but they're not. They're little files that are assigned a picture and tied to the programs they represent with the location of where that file can be found on your computer. That way you don't have to go digging for it and you don't have to know more about the workings of your computer's file system than you really want to. You just click it and it does what you need. They aren't the actual programs, though they might as well be for most people, and for all practicality they serve the same purpose. They have no real function apart from the program they're tied to, but because they are tied to that program they become powerful yet simple little tools that save everyone who uses them additional headaches (because normal computer use gives us enough of those).

What do Desktop shortcuts have to do with the Holy Eucharist? Bear with me, I'm getting to it.

The death of Jesus Christ on the Cross was the one great final sacrifice for all mankind. This is agreed upon by every Christian denomination and the acceptance of this fact is the most basic belief of the Church, however the Church's theologians debate it. The Scriptures and the Tradition of the Church dictate that one must partake of the Sacrifice of Jesus Christ in some way in order to receive salvation. This is true for any denomination, regardless of how this is interpreted by the individual denomination's theology.

We in the Western world, especially in the twenty-first century, are almost two thousand years removed from the kind of sacrificial religious practice that was well understood in the ancient Mediterranean world. When we hear that Christ became a sacrifice for us, we don't fully understand what was involved in the process and ritual of sacrifice.

Regarding the Passover sacrifice, for example, Exodus 12:5-10, 13 is the passage to look at. Verses 8-10 are the most relevant to this discussion:

"That same night they shall eat its roasted flesh with unleavened bread and bitter herbs. It shall not be eaten raw or boiled, but roasted whole with its head and shanks and inner organs. None of it must be kept beyond the next morning; whatever is left over in the morning shall be burned up." (WEB)

Where the Passover sacrifice was concerned, in both the original Passover and the celebration of the Passover meal, the sacrifice had to be eaten, and what was left over burned to ashes. The Passover was not valid and was ineffective if this regulation wasn't carried out. These same instructions were repeated for the Sin, Guilt, Peace, and Ordination sacrifices in Leviticus: Leviticus 6:19, 22-23 - Sin Offerings; Leviticus 7:6-7, 14-17, 28-38 - Guilt Offerings, Peace Offerings; Leviticus 8:31-32 - Ordination Sacrifices; Leviticus 10:16-18 – need of the High Priest to eat the sin offering.

Leviticus 7:15-17 speaks of the regulations regarding the peace/thanksgiving offering which, unlike the sin and guilt offerings, may have been eaten by "all who are clean," whereas the sin and guilt offerings were the exclusive domain of the males of the priestly line, and in particular of the priest who made atonement with the sacrifice:

"The flesh of the thanksgiving sacrifice shall be eaten on the day it is offered; none of it may be kept till the next day. However, if the sacrifice is a votive or a free will offering, it should indeed be eaten on the next day. Should any flesh from the sacrifice be left over on the third day, it must be burned up in the fire." (WEB)

These passages all describe the regulations for eating and otherwise dealing with the guilt, sin, and peace offerings. It could be argued that the sacrifices did not have to be eaten, they could have just been cremated. Leviticus 10:16-18 deals with the seriousness of the necessity of eating it as opposed to just burning it all:

"When Moses inquired about the goat of the sin offering, he discovered that it had all been burned. So he was angry with the surviving sons of Aaron, Eleazar and Ithamar, and said, 'Why did you not eat the sin offering in the sacred place, since it is most sacred? It has been given to you that you might bear the guilt of the community and make atonement for them before the LORD. If its blood was not brought into the inmost part of the sanctuary, you should certainly have eaten the offering in the sanctuary, in keeping with the command I had received.'" (WEB)

Hebrews 10:11-12 states that Jesus' death was a legitimate sacrifice under the Law:

"Every priest stands daily at his ministry, offering frequently those same sacrifices that can never take away sins. But this one offered one sacrifice for sins, and took his seat forever at the right hand of God."

And also in 9:12:

" . . . he entered once for all into the sanctuary, not with the blood of goats and calves but with his own blood, thus obtaining eternal redemption." (WEB)

So, if Jesus' death on the cross was a sacrifice, and this was the ancient understanding of sacrifices, what does that mean? In order for His death to be considered a valid and genuine sacrifice, it has to be partaken of. To partake in His sacrifice means to physically eat His flesh. He knew this and so did the people of His day. The people in John who questioned how they were supposed to eat His flesh and drink His blood didn't misunderstand Him. He meant what He said and they knew it, and it probably appalled them. Human sacrifices hadn't been practiced for centuries in that part of the world, and then only by pagan cultures which had been deliberately destroyed by God for that reason, among many. It had never been carried out by devout Jews; much less advocated by the prophets of Yahweh.

So, there was a problem. How was Jesus supposed to be a valid sacrifice for everyone who partakes of Him, when eating human beings was, and still is, culturally and morally abhorrent? And how was His sacrifice supposed to be made available for everyone who believes in Him long after the fact, especially after the resurrection?

Jesus Himself told us that solution. On the night He was betrayed, He took bread, blessed it, broke it and gave it to His disciples saying, "this is My Body which is broken for you." In the same way He took the cup, blessed it and gave it to His students saying, "this is My Blood of the Covenant which is shed for you and for many for the remission of sins. Do this in memory of Me." As High Priest, He ate from the offering, and then His disciples ate from it as well.

1 Corinthians 10:18-21 is probably one of the strongest references Paul makes to his belief in the Eucharistic communion as a sacrifice and the real presence of our Lord:

"Look at Israel according to the flesh; are not those who eat the sacrifices participants in the altar? So what am I saying? That meat sacrificed to idols is anything? Or that an idol is anything? No, I mean that what they sacrifice, they sacrifice to demons, not to God, and I do not want you to become participants with demons. You cannot drink the cup of the Lord and also the cup of demons. You cannot partake of the table of the Lord and of the table of demons." (WEB)

In the Greek religious system, it was also understood that where sacrifices to the gods were concerned, especially the twelve Olympians, they also were not completed until the sacrifice was eaten. Why would Paul get so upset about this if the communion wine and bread were only symbolic? Instead, his reaction is only natural if he believed that what was partaken as Eucharist was in fact the body and blood of Jesus Christ, and a sacrifice.

1 Corinthians 11:23-31 is the most prominent Pauline passage on Communion, and is even read during the communion held in

congregations who believe it to be only symbolic. But particular attention needs to be paid to verse 27 (WEB): "Therefore whoever eats the bread or drinks the cup unworthily will have to answer for the body and blood of the Lord." Why would any Christian have to answer for His body and blood if His body and blood are not actually involved?

This has been a point of division among Church theologians for centuries now. The ancient view was without debate: they accepted what Jesus said at face value and defended it without reservation. All those who refused to accept that the bread and wine were His Body and Blood were excommunicated as heretics. It was that simple, and that serious to them:

Ignatius, Bishop of Antioch, c. 105 AD:

"Take heed, then, to have only one Eucharist. For there is one flesh of our Lord Jesus Christ, and one cup to the unity of His blood."

"They [the Gnostics] abstain from the Eucharist and from prayer, because they do not believe the Eucharist to be the flesh of our Savior Jesus Christ . . . Those therefore who speak against this gift of God, incur death."

Irenaeus, Bishop of Lyons, c. 180 AD:

"Our opinion is in accordance with the Eucharist, and, in turn, the Eucharist establishes our opinion. For we offer to Him His own, announcing consistently the fellowship and union of the flesh and spirit. For the bread, which is produced from the earth, when it receives the invocation of God, is no longer common bread, but the Eucharist--consisting of two realities, earthly and heavenly. So also our bodies, when they receive the Eucharist, are no longer corruptible, having the hope of the resurrection to eternity."

"But if the flesh does not obtain salvation, then neither did the Lord redeem us with His blood, nor is the cup of the Eucharist the communion of His blood, nor is the bread which we break the communion of His body."

"He has acknowledged the cup (which is a part of the creation) as His own blood, from which He refreshes our blood. And the bread (also part of the creation) He has established as His own body, from which He gives increase to our bodies. When, therefore, the mingled cup and the baked bread receive the word of God, and the Eucharist of the blood and the body of Christ is made . . . how can they [the Gnostics] maintain that the flesh is incapable of receiving the gift of God."

"The wine and bread having received the Word of God, become the Eucharist, which is the body and blood of Christ."

Clement of Alexandria, theologian and mentor of Origen, c. 195 AD:

"To drink the blood of Jesus is to become partaker of the Lord's immortality . . . As wine is blended with water, so is the Spirit with man . . . And the mixture of both—of the water and of the word—is called the Eucharist, renowned and glorious grace. Those who by faith partake of it are sanctified both in body and soul."

Tertullian, Apologist in North Africa, c. 207 AD:

"He declared plainly enough what He meant by the bread, when He called the bread His own body. He likewise, when mentioning the cup and making the new testament to be sealed in His blood, affirmed the reality of His body."

Origen, presbyter and theologian, c. 248 AD:

"We also eat the bread presented to us. And this bread becomes by prayer a sacred body, which sanctifies those who sincerely partake of it."

Cyprian, Bishop of Carthage in North Africa, c. 250 AD:

"He says that whoever will eat of His bread will live forever. So it is clear that those who partake of His body and receive the Eucharist by right of communion are living. On the other hand, we must fear and pray lest anyone who is separate from Christ's body—being barred from communion—should remain at a distance from salvation. For He Himself warns and says, 'Unless you eat the flesh of the Son of man and drink His blood, you have no life in you.'"

"Certainly, only the priest who imitates that which Christ did [i.e. using wine mixed with water] is the one who truly discharges the office of Christ. He only offers a true and full sacrifice in the church to God the Father when he proceeds to offer it in the manner that he sees Christ Himself to have offered it."

Justin Martyr, apologist, c. 160 AD:

"He then speaks of those Gentiles, namely us, who in every place offer sacrifices to Him, i.e. the bread of the Eucharist, and also the cup of the Eucharist."

These days, many churches hold differing views ranging from the literal body and blood of Christ to only a representation of the body and blood of Christ. Such views hold names like transubstantiation, consubstantiation, and others. The central debate is the fact that once consecrated, the bread and wine remain, to all experience of the senses, bread and wine. They don't look any different and they don't taste any different. Certainly not like the metallic taste of human blood, or the taste of human flesh.

I'm going to run the risk of being yelled at and propose that the bread and wine was and remains a similar solution to the desktop shortcut. The bread and wine themselves are in fact just bread and wine until they are Sacramentally linked to the one sacrifice of Jesus Christ on the cross, and once they are linked, they are linked permanently. This link which crosses time and space to one event in history keeps us from having to develop time travel and physically eat the dead body of Jesus Christ. It allows us to partake in His sacrifice in a real and powerful way under circumstances that would render it otherwise impossible to access for anyone, even His disciples who were contemporary with Him.

In the end, I don't think it's all that important as to how this is done or how we explain it. The desktop shortcut is only an analogy, and not everyone may relate. The important thing is that the bread and wine become so intertwined with the body and blood of Jesus Christ as to become indistinguishable from the corpse removed from the cross two thousand years ago, and we should thank God that they do. It's an "application launcher" that defies all explanation, and is rightly called a "mystery." It is the mercy and love of God at work shielding us to some degree from the gruesome reality of the mechanics of His sacrifice, a constant reminder of that sacrifice for us, and it is also a reminder of our death with Him.

As we prepare to celebrate the Holy Eucharist on this Sunday or a Sunday soon, even if you only call it Communion, let's remember what it really is, and Who.

7 | A Ramble about Saints

I've been to a number of funerals in my life. I've said goodbye to more family and friends than I wanted. I've said goodbye to grandparents, classmates, teachers, and people I only met in passing. I had to say goodbye to a man not that much younger than myself who, when he was in a great deal of pain, the Lord had led me to guide him back to Him. For that young man, I had to mourn his passing on my own as I wasn't able to attend his memorial. As I try to count the number of funerals I have been to, I realize I can't remember how many of them I've attended. But I remember the images of them quite well.

Some of them I knew very well, others only in passing. Some of them were quite lavish and extravagant, such as a police officer's funeral in which I had the privilege to take part. Others were very quiet, with very few people in attendance, such as my great grandmother's. Some were solemn, but without faith; remembering the person's life and understanding that their life was now permanently gone. Others were more of a quiet celebration. I remember my Grandma Claudia's funeral, my paternal grandmother. The sense there was not that she was gone, but simply transformed and gone home.

Here soon, I will attend another. A dear friend, for whom I was not there when she needed me at the end. That's a regret I will likely not get over soon. We will go, remember her with words, praise the Lord with song, and then spread the ashes of her physical form out into the ocean, as she wanted. And then we will go home, acknowledging that we will see her again . . . someday.

The Scriptures say that all who are baptized into Christ Jesus are joined to Him. That we are all knit together as One Body, one organism (as one of my professors once said in class); joined together by the Holy Spirit in a permanent, unbreakable bond. It also says that those who are absent from the body are present with the Lord, and that death no longer has any meaning for those of us who are in Christ Jesus. It says, "O grave where is your victory, O death where is your sting?" According to Paul, death is absolutely meaningless for those who are in Christ Jesus. It is a momentary annoyance at worst, and a release and transformation at best.

Why then do we act as though we actually believe that they're gone? If death means nothing to the body of Christ, if we really believe this, why do we assume that they're actually dead and treat the grave as this insurmountable chasm across which we lose the communion of our brothers and sisters until "someday?" Is this what He died for? To merely give us the faint hope of seeing them again "someday," or to keep us bound together in His spirit as a part of His Eternal Life, sharing His Eternal Life as one organism? If we honestly don't believe we're connected to them anymore or that the grave still has some power over us, why do we profess faith in Jesus Christ at all? What good does it do? If we are truly separated by death from our brothers and sisters, then the cross has failed. God Forbid It!

The resurrection begins with our death to ourselves and is completed upon the death of our physical bodies. Those who have passed in Christ are not dead but have begun their final transformation outside of time and space as we know it. They are not separated from us, but are integrally a part of us through Him. They are still family. They are still our brothers and sisters. And as the scriptures indicate in the letter to the Hebrews and in the

Revelation of John, they know perfectly well what's going on with us, and are a great cloud of witnesses watching us run our races. What's more, do we honestly believe that knowing these things, as family who care about us, that they're going to stand idly by and watch us as spectators, or, as family, are they going to be caring about us, interceding for us and praying for us?

What would we do in their place? What do we do now? Do I stop caring about and praying for my brothers and sisters in Christ simply because I've had my skin and bones removed? Truth is, it would make more sense to me that having my skin and bones removed would free me to love and intercede for them even more directly in His presence. Rather than prohibit me, it would free and embolden me to experience the ever present Reality that is Him, and us in Him.

"Not for these only do I pray, but for those also who believe in me through their word, that they may all be one; even as you, Father, are in me, and I in you, that they also may be one in us; that the world may believe that you sent me. The glory which you have given me, I have given to them; that they may be one, even as we are one; I in them, and you in me, that they may be perfected into one; that the world may know that you sent me, and loved them, even as you loved me." (John 17:20-23, WEB) This was the prayer of Jesus Christ. Do we honestly think the Father said "no?"

John, Paul, Peter, Mary, Andrew, and all those who came before us are just as much our brothers and sisters now as they were thousands of years ago. They are still a part of our family. Those who physically die in Christ are not dead, but are living, and this physical death itself is only a momentary pause. The suggestion that they can't hear us, don't know what's happening with us, don't pray for us, or don't care, is itself unbiblical and runs against what the Church has taught since the beginning. It is also, quite frankly, insulting to our brothers and sisters who are with Him at the moment.

The thought of this threatens many, and threatens the faith and theology of many. It used to threaten mine. Communion with the dead? Isn't that being a medium? Not if those people are not truly dead, but have passed from this dying body into Life in His presence.

Those who have died outside of Christ are outside of Christ and are not a part of the body. They are dead, and awaiting judgment. I honestly can't speak for the Lord in this matter, because I'm not Him, and only He really knows what their fate will be. I only know that they are not bound to each other as we are through His Spirit, and they are not joined in His death and resurrection as we are through His Spirit.

Jesus said this:

"But concerning the resurrection of the dead, haven't you read that which was spoken to you by God, saying, 'I am the God of Abraham, and the God of Isaac, and the God of Jacob?' God is not the God of the dead, but of the living." (Matthew 22:31-32, WEB)

If we believe in the resurrection, and if we believe in Jesus Christ, then we must accept all that goes with it. We must act on all that goes with it. And, in doing so, we can rejoice that our brothers and sisters who have gone before us are waiting for us to join them with open arms, and also extend those open arms now in the Spirit when we need them. That's what brothers and sisters are for. That's what family is for.

8 | Concerning Bible Versions . . .

There was a time when I was in college that I became very concerned about which Bible I should be using. I didn't want to use one based on the wrong Greek text (or Hebrew for that matter) because I was taught that certain Greek texts were corrupted and had "taken away" from scripture. Certain Bible translations were watered down and could be used to teach heresy. I was very careful, and eventually came to be able to actually read the Greek text for myself (not so much the Hebrew, I was always more of a Greek geek), because it seemed like no English translation could be trusted. I even undertook to make several translations of portions of the New Testament myself.

I can now honestly say that I've been studying Greek for over twenty years. I've read numbers of different Bible translations, and added to those numbers with my own manuscripts. I have come to several conclusions about this whole matter about which Bible translation is better.

In short, the best version of the Bible is the one you can understand. After comparing the Greek and English for years, my conclusion is that most translations, regardless of the source text, say pretty much what the Greek text says, inasmuch as they can. Can you get more out of the straight Greek text? Yes, if you take the time to learn to read ancient Greek as fluently as possible; but if you don't then use a translation that speaks your language.

If your particular version of theology absolutely depends on a certain translation of a certain passage of scripture, then there's something wrong. If your theology can't stand up to a modern English reading of a passage, but has to have a 400 year old dialect of English in order for it to work, there's something wrong and you need to rethink what you're teaching or being taught.

I've encountered the King James Version only fan club repeatedly over the years, ever since Bible School. I even tried to make nice with it. But it makes absolutely no sense that people would be adamant that they must use this version and no other. I have heard again and again that it's "Peter and Paul's version." Some people who use this expression are actually serious. This is disturbing and ignorant. If you want St. Paul's version, use the Greek text. If you really want to use the Bible which Peter and Paul used, then use the Greek Septuagint version of the Old Testament.

The truth is that such people, as I once was, are so concerned about having their Biblical theology right that they ignore what that very same Bible actually teaches about mercy, Grace, love, forgiveness, and compassion. This is unacceptable.

Right now, I have a combination New King James Version/ St. Athanasius Academy Septuagint Bible which I absolutely love using. It's as close to the Bible Peter and Paul used as I'm going to get in an English translation. My wife hates the New King James and uses the New Living Translation, which we use with the kids because they don't understand a word of my Bible. When I really want to read or study something, I go to the Greek. I've given *The Message* to a dear friend who had trouble understanding the Bible, and she loved it. My Mom still uses the New International Version, and doesn't want to switch to anything else. I've read through the Jewish New Testament, The Unvarnished New Testament, Tyndale's New Testament, and others, and I received some good insights from the translators' work on all of them. The version rarely matters, but it is whether or not the person reading it understands what it says. If they don't, then it's a worthless book to them.

Sadly, and I'll only comment on this briefly, this dispute arises because of the teaching of Sola Scriptura, that Scripture alone is necessary for understanding all matters of theology, doctrine, dogma, and faith. Because there are more than a few who refuse to admit that the Gospel of Jesus Christ is handed down to us by more than just Holy Scripture, they must make absolutely certain that the version of the Bible people use is the one which says what they want it to say in the way they want it said, and condemn all others as being "less than" or twisted Scripture. They adopt the same attitude as some of the Reformers who would have preferred if some books of the New Testament, such as the "General Epistle of James," had been left out. This is one of the more negative legacies of the Reformation. When they abandoned the Sacred Tradition of the Church, it became "every man did what was right in his own eyes."

The preacher who tells you that you're using the wrong Bible doesn't understand the Gospel. He doesn't understand it in the slightest. The Church today is filled with such clergy. This is the truly twisted and frightening thing.

9 | A Ramble about Creation

I don't think I've ever written a ramble directly about this subject. I just started mulling it over again in my mind after reading an article in *Scientific American* online, and then reading some of the responses in the article from other well meaning Christians.

The book of Genesis says that God created the world in six days. Modern science says that the universe, the planet, and all life on it took billions of years to form. This is *the* classic argument between those of us who believe the Holy Scriptures and those of us who read and keep up with modern scientific study, theories, and advances in understanding. There's a lot of good research and evidence that indicates that modern science has a more correct view of the timeline involved, and yet the Bible is the inspired word of God, and whether or not we accept the doctrine of "Sola Scriptura," there are few professing Christians who will declare the Bible to be somehow wrong (myself included).

Thus began the great war of words between Bible believing Christians and sincere scientists ("The Bible says this!" and "But the data says this!"). The great conflict between general and special revelation. The question then becomes, if both means of revelation are given by God, how can they contradict each other?

I remember reading a couple of books by a Dr. Hugh Ross, *The Fingerprint of God* and *The Creator and the Cosmos*. Dr. Ross is an astrophysicist who is also a professing Christian. He wrote that the order of the six days of creation reads like watching the formation of the earth and evolutionary history from the viewpoint of someone standing on the earth. There are many who have taken a similar standpoint, putting forth ideas such as each "day" of creation actually being an "evolutionary age" of time.

I would like to go back and expand on Dr. Ross' observation and suggest that what Genesis is describing is not six literal 24 hour days of "creation," but it is describing six literal 12 hour periods of revelation about creation. Genesis itself gives us the clue to this as it describes, literally, "there is evening and there is morning, day one, . . . day two, . . . day three," etc. Moses is describing being shown something for twelve hours at a time, and then given twelve hours to process what he has seen and get some sleep before the next round. There is a passage in Exodus (24:15-17) which describes a separate six day period, prior to the forty days and forty nights, when Moses was on the mountain alone with God, which sounds an awful lot like it might be related in some way to Genesis 1.

Here is my humble opinion on the dispute. Moses was on the mountain for a six-day period prior to his forty-day stint according to Exodus. During those six days, God took that time to reveal millions of years of His creative acts. Being God, He showed it to Moses from Moses' viewpoint on the ground in a kind of "fast forward," as much as his human mind could assimilate and process at a time, and then it all amalgamated in his mind as Moses attempted to absorb and retain all of it. He then wrote down the gist of what he could remember. The point of the first chapter of Genesis then becomes not *how* God created the world, but *that* He created the world.

How is it that we have gotten to the point that a Christian's personal faith and relationship with God is so fragile that it depends on a specific, yet scientifically problematic, interpretation of Holy Scripture? How is it that we have gotten to the point that entire theologies of salvation are dependent on a specific translation or understanding of a particular word in a single verse in Hebrew or Greek?

I find it fascinating that there is good archaeological evidence that the beginnings of civilization arose between six and seven thousand years ago near Tabriz, Iran and southern Georgia. This is the best location I have ever heard for the geographical site of the Biblical Garden of Eden (believe it or not, it matches perfectly with the Biblical description of where Eden was located). I find it just as fascinating that human beings most likely started wearing clothes about 150,000 years ago (roughly when the body louse evolved). I also find it fascinating that Neanderthals actually died out between thirty and fifty thousand years ago and were not genetically related or descended from modern Homo Sapiens. I find all this information fascinating, and it adds to my understanding of Genesis. It doesn't compete with or contradict that understanding.

I think God told us what he considered important in the Holy Scriptures. I also think there's a lot He didn't say; whole chapters of human history which He refused to elaborate on because He didn't think it necessary for His purposes to tell us. These are Chapters, some of them quite dark, which we get small glimmers of through archaeological and paleontological research. Some of which chapters are likely better left buried in the past from what I have read. This doesn't make Him a liar under any circumstances, but it does make Him far more prudent than ourselves in what he chooses to reveal directly.

The important realization of our human history that Genesis tells us is that somewhere in our distant past, our ancestors disobeyed God and passed down a disorder that keeps us from knowing Him without His direct intervention. The next important realization is the constant direct intervention by God in our history so that we would come to know Him in spite of our disorder.

If we are continuously fighting about how much time (a concept which is meaningful only to human beings) God took to create the world, were are limiting God and missing the real message of Holy Scripture through this meaningless distraction. This message is that

God wants to help us and has been working without a break to do so. These divisive stands can only be described as the very definition of heresy. They only serve to distract from the Gospel, and from Jesus Christ Himself.

Part VI | The Church, and How We Treat Each Other

1 | A Ramble about Lost Sheep

Some time ago, as I was pulling one-ton pallets through the crowded aisles of the "big box store" I worked at, I got this image in my head from the Lord.

There was a rancher who owned a lot of sheep, and shepherds were hired to watch over different flocks. Some flocks were larger, some were smaller, but all the sheep belonged ultimately to the rancher, not the individual shepherd in charge of them.

Some of the shepherds were doing their job well and faithfully. The sheep were well cared for, and the shepherds had the exhaustion and bags under their eyes to prove it. Other shepherds however were not. Some beat the sheep under their care. Some didn't feed them properly. Others overfed them but then didn't exercise them. Some were abused in other ways, or poisoned because the shepherd didn't seem to know the difference between good feed and bad. Some shepherds were fleecing the sheep far too often, and as such they were sick and ill prepared for the winter.

As a result, some sheep broke from their flocks and stalls and ran for the hills, terrified of the shepherds that were over them. Out in the hills, some of them were able to survive on their own and were doing okay for the most part. Others however got into poisonous plants. Some couldn't traverse the terrain and were injured, many of them quite seriously. Others ate themselves over cliffs, as sheep are quite capable of doing.

And as I saw this in my head, I could sense the concern the Rancher had for his sheep that had fled. I could also sense the anger that he had towards the shepherds in question, to whom He had entrusted His livestock. And I sensed from Him that someone needed to go get them and look after them.

I have since wrestled with this question. How? If we were talking literal sheep, one could take a tranquilizer gun and some rope and go collect them. Unfortunately, it's not quite that easy with the Lord's sheep. It would be nice if it was, but it isn't. Often, those who have been hurt or abused tend to run from anyone who looks or smells like a shepherd. And honestly, I would too if I had been abused like that. Come to think of it, I have run once or twice myself.

One thought which has run through my mind lately is that these are the people for whom Jesus targeted His ministry. He didn't target the unbeliever (read Gentile), and He didn't target those who were professedly religious (read Pharisee, Sadducee, Essene, or other). He said instead, "I was not sent except to the lost (lit. ruined) sheep of the house of Israel," (Matthew 15:24) and also, "When Jesus heard it, he said to them, 'Those who are healthy have no need for a physician, but those who are sick do. But you go and learn what this means: "I desire mercy, and not sacrifice," for I came not to call the righteous, but sinners to repentance.'"(Matthew 9:12-13, WEB)

So what do we do about these brothers and sisters in Christ, many who are baptized, who believe in Jesus Christ, yet do not trust the Church or its shepherds? Do we just write them off? Do we let them just go elsewhere? Do we let them fall off of cliffs? After talking with some pastors (several of whom I respect highly), it seems like that is the general attitude. It's their fault for not accepting the authority of the Church or the local churches' pastors.

Another thing about these lost sheep, is that many of them seem to be my generation and younger. I was talking to an old friend of mine recently who happens to be a youth pastor. The church he serves at has lost a lot of the people (including myself) who had been in the youth group over a decade ago and now are in their late twenties or early thirties. I could sense from him that he had a real heart for them, but he too seems to be at a loss as to how to bring them back into a regular church attendance of some, or any, kind. After putting out an inquiry to various churches in the area, he said that the general response he got was "good luck with that."

These are the people who are most on the heart of Jesus Christ: the members of the family who have somehow been ruined and written off by the Church either intentionally or unintentionally. These are the people He went after Himself while on earth, and I believe these are the people we need to go after and take care of. But the question remains, "How?"

2 | A Ramble about an Unacceptable Situation

There is a question that is never far from my mind and usually running in the background somewhere. How do we fix the Church of Jesus Christ?

This assumes that somehow it's broken, or somehow disordered. Whether or not you agree with me that it is . . . we can argue rings around each other why it is or isn't, and get nowhere.

But I see symptoms of a much greater problem. I have previously written about the "judgmentalism" of various professing Christians, when Jesus Christ taught non-judgment. I have previously written about these lost sheep who have run from the Church, and whose faith exists in various states of ruin. Often, the members of the visible Church, because of their hypocrisy, are the cause of those outside of the Church not wanting to become members. Why would anyone want to follow Jesus Christ when we don't follow Him ourselves? Why would anyone profess faith when professing Christians often betray their lack of faith by their actions? The One, Holy, Universal, and Apostolic Church of Jesus Christ is fractured into a thousand and tens of thousands of bickering parties, each professing that they alone have the real "Truth." And this "Truth" which they profess is a theological doctrine or dogma which takes all precedence in terms of importance over what Jesus Christ actually taught. In some cases it takes precedence even over Jesus Christ Himself. In the more extreme versions, murder is even committed in His Name.

The *Tao Te Ching*, in the first "chapter," says this:

When the Way is lost, afterward comes integrity.

When integrity is lost, afterward comes humaneness.

When humaneness is lost, afterward comes righteousness.

When righteousness is lost, afterward comes etiquette.

In short, what it means is that when "the Way" is lost, one's religious practice and belief devolves into nothing more than a facade of empty, polite niceties and etiquette. Here "righteousness" refers to the belief in the righteousness of one's actions or beliefs.

The Buddhist would likely agree that when "the Truth" is lost, there is only ignorance and self. We act on only what we can see, feel, smell, taste, and hear. These things are constantly changing around us. We become locked into our own desires and attachments, and we become lost in the sea of transient and impermanent experiences.

I would argue that when "the Life" is lost, there remains only the onset of decay to the body. At first it appears as attractive and healthy as it was when the Life was within it, but as each second passes by with no blood flow, it begins to rot and stink and decay as it breaks down. Then it is evident to all that what is present is a dead corpse and not a living body.

The Way, the Truth, and the Life is Jesus Christ. He told us what would happen if we don't remain in Him as a branch remains in the vine. We could do nothing. Much worse, the branch would wither and die and be thrown into a fire where it would be consumed (John 15:4-6).

What then is the answer to this problem? I thought at one time possibly starting another congregation or another church. But the truth is that would only add to the problem, not correct it. Others saw the same problem in the Church's history and responded with new denominations and sects and reform movements. They responded with new theologies, believing that the old theologies were the problem to be corrected. If new teachings or new Churches were the answer, then the problem would have been corrected a long time ago, a thousand times over.

It is like the illustration of Plato's cave *(The Republic,* Book VII). This is an illustration that the Greek philosopher Plato used around twenty-five hundred years ago. In it, a group of people are chained in a cave in such a way so as all they can see are the shadows of things on a wall, not even being able to turn and look at one another. As a result, they believe that the shadows are the reality. When a man is freed from his chains, and escapes the cave, he sees the sun, real grass, and real objects for the first time. In the illustration, he then goes back and tries to explain his discovery to those still chained, who then think he is insane. A more modern retelling of this illustration would be the movie *Matrix,* where people believe that the reality they are experiencing is the real world when, in fact, it is a computer generated simulation run and administered by machine overlords. Those from the real world plug back in, attempting to free those people still trapped in the virtual world.

The difference from Plato's illustration is that those who may have been freed from the cave to experience the sunlight have instead chosen to be shackled again to the cave. They choose to lock themselves into seeing only the shadows, all the while proclaiming that they are free when any fool who can see the shadows can tell that they are not. Or it is like someone being freed from the Matrix voluntarily choosing to plug himself back into the pod he escaped from and submit to his machine overlords, all the while declaring himself to be free of both.

We have, collectively if not individually, lost far more than the Truth which Jesus Christ taught. We have lost Jesus Christ Himself, and have willingly chosen to be blinded again by the god of this world. We need to recover the Way, the Truth, and the Life who is Jesus Christ. This can't be done through more theology, more division, more Bible Studies, Church meetings, sermons, rallies, tent revivals, books that don't get read except by pastors, or any other tactic which has been tried. We all can see the need unless we're totally blinded. We know something is malfunctioning or disordered somewhere. We can see the evidence for it ourselves, but we can't put our finger on it. It's just out of the range of our perception. So, we shrug our shoulders and go back to doing what we were doing.

We need Jesus Christ. We, the Church, need Jesus Christ. We need Him. We need to be wrapped in Him. We need to live and breathe Him. We need to eat, drink, dream, and live Jesus Christ. St. Paul wrote, "Or don't you know that all we who were baptized into Christ Jesus have been baptized into His death . . . ?" (Romans 6:3, WEB) And also, "For you have died, and your life is hidden with Christ in God. When Christ who is your life appears, then you also will appear with Him in glory." (Colossians 3:3-4, ESV)

We don't need any or more theologies or books about Him. We don't need to discuss Him. We don't need to do things in His name. We don't need to act for Him in His absence. All these things are good, and at times necessary, but all are worthless without Him. Fundamentally, we need Him. We need Him flowing through us. We need Him flowing through veins, filling our lungs, running up and down our nerves. We need Him within us and pouring out through us. When He is not present, then we decay and become blinded. The Buddha said, "There is Self and there is Truth, where Self is, Truth is not. Where Truth is, Self is not." Jesus Christ is Truth, and where He is, there is no "self" to turn inward to. At the same time, where "self" is present, Jesus Christ is not, and we must understand this simple fact.

The Church collectively, especially in the Western world, is a decaying corpse. One of the things God is really good at is resurrection, but resurrection only comes through Jesus Christ. Resurrection only comes when one dies to self and is integrally joined to Jesus Christ in His death. Unless self dies, Jesus Christ will not come in resurrection.

We have, collectively, lost what it means to be Christian: to follow Jesus Christ in His death and resurrection. Very few, it seems, have individually found it. This is an unacceptable situation.

3 | The Prime Directive

If you're like me and grew up on Star Trek in one or more of it's many incarnations, you know exactly what I mean when I say "the prime directive." It's so ingrained into the fabric of the Star Trek universe and culture that anyone who has ever watched any part of Star Trek (film or television) instinctively knows what it is without having to go back and review which episode or movie from which it came.

For those of you who were not on a Star Trek I.V. drip for most of their lives, let me explain. The Prime Directive is Starfleet General Order Number One, and according to *Wikipedia.org* (under the article title of "Prime Directive"):

"The Prime Directive states

"As the right of each sentient species to live in accordance with its normal cultural evolution is considered sacred, no Starfleet personnel may interfere with the normal and healthy development of alien life and culture. Such interference includes introducing superior knowledge, strength, or technology to a world whose society is incapable of handling such advantages wisely. Starfleet personnel may not violate this Prime Directive, even to save their lives and/ or their ship, unless they are acting to right an earlier violation or an accidental contamination of said culture. This directive takes precedence over any and all other considerations, and carries with it the highest moral obligation. (Giancarlo Genta, Lonely Minds in the Universe: The Search for Extraterrestrial Intelligence, Springer, 2007, p. 208.)"

"Nothing within these articles of Federation shall authorize the United Federation of Planets to intervene in matters which are essentially the domestic jurisdiction of any planetary social system, or shall require the members to submit such matters to settlement under these Articles of Federation; But this principle shall not prejudice the application of enforcement measures under Chapter VII. (STAR TREK TECHNICAL MANUAL [TOS], [Articles of the Federation, Chapter I, Article II, Paragraph VII])"

Within the Star Trek universe the Prime Directive is absolutely sacrosanct, and violating it brings severe consequences. Not the least of these consequences is that the Starfleet officer who violates it is considered to have committed a gross atrocity in the process. The idea behind it is simple, they don't want to cause irreparable harm to any culture or society that isn't ready to accept the realities an interstellar civilization and alliance would bring. The parallels in real history are numerous as European civilization repeatedly interfered with the natural development of indigenous cultures with the result of many of those cultures and languages being lost, and often their people ending in a worse position than if they had been left alone.

As Christians we have also been given instructions by Jesus Christ and His Apostles that are very similar to the Prime Directive. As I have watched the protests on the news this week surrounding the President's commencement speech, I have been reminded of this. There have been protesters now on both sides of the abortion debate, both pro-life and pro-choice, marching and demonstrating, most notably on the pro-life side against the President's appearance at a Catholic University because of his politically pro-choice stance. People have argued, been arrested, carried signs, and even held a competing graduation ceremony for those students opposed to the President's presence.

The Church Fathers spoke out against the practice of abortion as far back as the Roman Empire. I find it intriguing that an issue that was debated two millennia ago is still relevant today. It has always been the view of the Church that all life is sacred, and that the termination of the life of a child, whether in the womb or out of it, is an atrocity. I do not disagree.

But where our Prime Directive kicks in is that this is our belief. This is our standard. This is a view and belief of the kingdom and government of heaven, and applies to all those within that kingdom. As St. Paul wrote in 1st Corinthians 5:12-13, "For what have I to do with judging outsiders? Is it not those inside the church whom you are to judge? God judges those outside. 'Purge the evil person from among you.'" (ESV)

We cannot take the direction and governance of the Holy Spirit on such matters and enforce it on those outside the Church. It would be the same as if the United States decided that it was going to enforce the US Constitution on Mexico, by force if necessary. Mexico is not a part of the United States and it would be a grossly inappropriate attack on their sovereignty, whether or not we believe our laws to be of a higher moral quality than theirs.

We're not here to enforce an artificial and unsustainable moral conduct on those who are not conjoined to Jesus Christ and not possessed of His Holy Spirit. The attempts to do so only lead to more suffering, guilt, anger, and frustration on the part of all parties involved. The choice to follow Jesus Christ is just that, a choice. Like Jesus Christ, we weren't called to follow Him to condemn the unsaved world, but that the world might be saved through Him with us as privileged participants in that salvation.

We are sent, like Him, to seek and save that which is lost, not to expect the spiritually blind to be able to live as though they can see. Even our own civil secular governments recognize the cruelty of that expectation. We're here to introduce them to a relationship with the Father through the Son by the power of the Holy Spirit. To bind up that which is broken and fan the smoldering match into a flame. Attempting to impose the conduct of the Church on the unbelieving only encourages and produces self-righteous hypocrisy at best. At worst it completely muddies the Gospel message into something unrecognizable and pushes people away from what they are told Christ and Christianity are supposed to be, making them unwilling to really seek Him as He is. It becomes the anti-Gospel, and a spirit of anti-Christ.

It just doesn't work.

There are many women who make the choice to have an abortion, for whatever reason. This is a choice that harms them and leaves them scarred for the rest of their lives. It's our responsibility and directive to care for them and have compassion on them. It's our express directive to neither judge nor condemn anyone outside the Church, but to offer forgiveness and healing, as Jesus Christ did for us.

This is our prime directive in interacting with the unbelieving world: "Don't judge, so that you won't be judged. Don't condemn, so that you won't be condemned. Forgive, and you will be forgiven . . . Love your enemies, do good to those who hate you, bless those who persecute you, and pray for those who abuse you and mistrust you . . . Love your neighbor as yourself . . . Love one another as I have loved you." It is absolutely sacred, and the consequences for violation can be eternal and devastating.

4 | A Ramble about "Judas"

I recently had the experience of watching a performance on Youtube of Lady Gaga's latest single, *Judas*. I had read about it and the controversy it was engendering on a news website and I was curious as to what was so offensive. I listened to the song, and then watched an interview where Lady Gaga explained where the inspiration for the song came from.

The song had to do with how she felt about an ex-boyfriend, or series of ex-boyfriends, who she felt had betrayed her. She explained that while she felt betrayed by that person she was also still in love with him, thus she was "still in love with Judas." The controversy came with the religious imagery, which at face value could be taken as extremely dark and disturbing.

As I watched the video and listened to the song, some thoughts occurred to me. Am I not like that? Judas could be seen as representative of the love or attraction to worldly things, and the selling out of being "in Christ" for the love of money, possessions, status, and all such things. When I choose to pursue those things instead of Christ, am I not still "in love with Judas?" Do I not still betray Jesus with a kiss when I pay lip service to Him, but my heart runs after empty things?

The other thought that occurs to me is this; is not Christ Himself still in love with Judas? Had Judas not hanged himself out of guilt, wouldn't He have restored him just as He restored Peter? Peter had also betrayed Him by denying three times that he even knew Him. Don't I do this too? Doesn't He restore me in the same way? There is little doubt that Judas is suffering in a hell of his own making, but that doesn't stop the love of God for him any more than it stopped the love of God for Peter. Peter just made a different choice. Feeling himself totally unworthy, he had chosen to go back to fishing when Jesus found him again and restored him.

There's a lot of malcontent towards Lady Gaga for this song and this video. I think it might be because it touches the nerve of a place we don't want to go or see within ourselves. I think that our anger is misdirected. Lady Gaga isn't a Saint, but she isn't any more of a sinner than I am, or anyone else for that matter. I think the reason why we want to throw stones is because we are trying to deceive ourselves into thinking we are without sin, or somehow better than she is. The last time someone tried to stone a prostitute in Jesus' presence, they had the good sense to drop the rocks and let her go when He challenged them to produce her accuser ("Let he who is without sin throw the first stone . . . "). Did we forget that He is still watching? We need to remember that as we judge, so are we also judged.

5 | A Ramble about Unity

"Cursed be that love and unity for whose sake the Word of God must be put to the stake." I wrote that quote from the Reformation down on the title page of my Bible as I took notes in class one day in Bible School. I hung on my professor's every word as he taught. I thought the sentiment was so very right, and I thought the Reformer who spoke it divinely inspired. The Reformer in question meant of course that there can be no love and unity with people who didn't subscribe to his interpretation of Holy Scripture. More literally, he also meant those who put the word of God to the stake by burning every vernacular (common language) translation of the Bible they could get their hands on in order to maintain power and control.

"I believe in One, Holy, Catholic, and Apostolic Church . . . " So says the Creed, agreed on by the whole Church at the Councils of Nicea and Constantinople, which many if not most churches recite every Sunday. The word "catholic" simply means "universal" or "general," and comes from the Greek word, "katholikos." All of us profess, even if we are unfamiliar with the Creed itself, in one

Universal Church of Jesus Christ, which is holy to God and a direct descendant of the work and teaching of the Apostles.

We generally agree that this Church consists of, at bare minimum, all those who have been baptized by faith into Jesus Christ. We also generally agree that all those within the Church are in fact brothers and sisters. To a somewhat more strained degree we generally agree that all those saints who came before us are both our spiritual ancestors, and continuous brothers and sisters in Christ. Some of the worst fighting comes between brothers and sisters, doesn't it? No one can hurt you more than members of your own family.

What creates the unity within a family are ties of kinship, and an understanding that those ties are more important than distance, culture, strong differences of opinion, or hurt feelings. A girl's brother may tease her relentlessly at home, but heaven help anyone else who dares to tease or hurt her at school. We understand, and we are brought up to understand, that we are to care about the members of our family and take care of them even if they are otherwise strangers to us. "Oh, by the way, your cousin Bob from Scotland, you know the one who was married to your second cousin Sally, three times removed on your great grandmother's side? Well he's coming to stay with us for a few days." Any protest to this is met with, "Well, he's family and he needs a place to stay." Nothing is more hurtful within a family than that family disowning one of its members. "You are no longer my son, and you are no longer welcome here."

Within the Family of Jesus Christ there are strong differences of opinion. These differences are mostly about things that we can neither see nor touch, or about things we have only heard about but for which we weren't there. Internal family squabbles have turned into blood feuds, similar to the Hatfields and the McCoys, that have gone on for so long that very few people even remember what we were feuding about. Those that do know what it's about only know because they've studied for years in order to be able to take sides in an educated manner.

I used to think that the reunification of this family, the end of all this infighting, could come. Now, I'm not so sure any more. We're all so concerned about being right, that we've forgotten that we're family. We've forgotten the central tenet of that family, and that's to love and care about one another.

Heresy quite literally means division. And a heretic, in the strictest sense of the word, is one who divides. The Apostles and the clergy who came after them cracked down on heretics because they were people who out of pride, ambition, or desire for money divided the Church, drawing people away in order to form their own congregations. This, first and foremost, was the unsound teaching they had to combat. They had to fight at all costs the breaking up of the family by selfish people. Somewhere along the line, this translated into an all out war on anyone with a different experience or interpretation, and this sentiment was then passed down through the centuries. Denomination to denomination, church to church, we simply do not tolerate anybody else's interpretation of theology. Except now, instead of the one, holy, catholic, and Apostolic Church being visibly one, holy, catholic, and apostolic; it appears (though in reality One Church) to be many Churches equally condemning each other as heretics.

Our unity will never come from theology. Theology literally means "the study of God." And while conforming with the larger body of accepted Truth, one's personal study of God will never be the same as the person next to him. One studies God by getting to know Him through one's personal experiences and deep prayer, as well as studying the experiences of others in the Holy Scriptures and the Church Fathers. God remains the same yesterday, today, and forever; but because we change and are different, our experiences of Him will change and be different. Even if He is not in motion, we are. This is why we argue and fight over teachings that, if you really look into them, are really different facets of the same Truth expressed semantically in different ways.

The only way the Church can be restored to visible unity is when we focus on the person, teaching, and practice of Jesus Christ, when we focus on Jesus Himself, and not teachings about Him. It can only be restored when we follow His teachings to love and care about everyone, including those who would be our enemies. The Scripture plainly says he who does not love, does not know God because God is love (1 John 4:8). It also says in 1 John 4:20 that, if you cannot love your brother whom you can see, how can you love God whom you cannot see? Jesus taught us to love God, one's brother, one's neighbor, and one's enemies. Where then is there room to hate anyone for those of us who profess to follow Him?

Finally, and I am as guilty of this as anyone, as family we must put the interests of that family over and above anything else. Blood is thicker than water it is said. No matter what happens with the government, or with politics, or with anything else, we can't let those things divide us as more important than our family. I would also argue that the blood of Jesus Christ should be thicker than any other.

Our road to unity is through remembering that we are all family. It was because we forgot that one central fact that we became divided and disowned one another. The Word of God teaches that love and unity is more important than whether, "I'm right and you're wrong." The interpretation of the Word of God that teaches otherwise is cursed.

6 | Back to the Basics

"Back to the Basics . . . Let's all get back to the basics." If I had a nickel for every time I heard that phrase I'd never need to work another day in my life. This phrase is used to try and re-orient people back to where they started so they can get a clearer perspective on where they're going and what they should do next. It's been a common enough catchphrase within business offices. On occasion you hear it within political campaigns. You also hear it frequently within churches. There often seem to be churches that start on their basics, and never leave them.

Here's a question. "What are the basics of the Christian faith?" This should be an easy question to answer for most of us who have been Christians, of one stripe or another, for most of our lives. What is the first thing that should be taught to new Christians and seekers of the faith of Jesus Christ?

I can count off of a list what is normally taught in most churches, or at least what people seem to pick up from their first encounters: conservative political activism, literal six day creationism, pro-life anti-abortionism, don't smoke, don't drink, don't have pre-marital sex, and "we don't associate with those people" who do. These are generally the first impressions people get when visiting churches (yes, this sounds harsh, but let's be honest with ourselves here). Interspersed throughout this, depending on the church and the pastor, maybe a Gospel message about turning to Jesus and accepting Jesus into your heart.

If those people stay to attend the church, they may go through discipleship classes which involve the doctrines of the Holy Trinity, man's sinfulness, Christ's death, burial and resurrection, Spiritual Gifts, tithing, the inerrancy of the Bible, End Times, and maybe things like baptism and holy communion might be covered, depending on the church. I am largely talking about Protestant churches here, although the Catholic Churches are not necessarily far behind on this matter if they teach anything at all outside of the homily; and let's face it, many don't. Generally, many churches don't stray too far from these topics.

So, these are the basics of the Christian faith. Are they? Are they really?

Why is it more important that people understand that God created the earth in six days than it is to understand what Jesus meant when He said "Don't judge so that you won't be judged, don't condemn so that you won't be condemned?" Why is it more important that new converts understand the importance of tithing than understanding what Jesus meant when he said, "If anyone wants to come after Me, let him deny himself, pick up his cross and follow Me."? And why is the goal of our salvation, the whole reason why we seek to follow Jesus Christ, i.e. union with God, considered theology too deep for most Christians to handle, and too much too soon for new converts?

It would seem to me that the basics of the faith ought to be the absolute minimum a person needs to know to progress in the faith. They should be the foundation on which a person can build his or her practice of Christianity and relationship with God. What good does it do a person if they fully understand the Holy Trinity (which is impossible by the way), yet have no tools on which to base a growing relationship with the Holy Trinity?

So, what would I consider to be the basics of the faith of Jesus Christ? In no particular order:

First: that which Jesus and his apostles taught was a relationship with God through Christ. The rules of the Christian religious life were put into place to foster that relationship, not to make people feel hopeless.

Second: the teachings of Jesus Christ. How can you claim to follow someone if you don't know what they are teaching? Furthermore, how can you follow someone if you don't put into practice what they taught? Jesus preached repentance. Jesus taught non-judgment. He taught forgiveness. He gave the command to love one another as He loved us. He taught non-retaliation, compassion, and love for one's enemies. The command to love and practice love was so important in the eyes of the Apostle John that he wrote that the person who does not love does not know God, because God is love. Jesus also taught detachment from possessions, trusting God for one's bodily provisions, and detachment from any relationship which becomes an obstacle to your relationship with God. If you look through the writings of the Apostles in the New Testament, they taught the exact same thing, and elaborated on it further.

What's deeply troubling is that the actual teaching of Jesus Christ is usually glossed over by most preachers today. It is consigned to the children's Sunday School because the adults have "deeper, more mature spiritual things" to learn. The truth is that people want excuses to not obey what He taught, or to not listen to it, and far too many preachers oblige them. This is a fundamentally dangerous way of thinking, especially since Jesus Himself warned against not doing what He taught.

Third: the union of the Christian with Jesus Christ in His death and resurrection through baptism. Mechanically speaking, this is the mechanism or foundation on which our salvation rests. This is what makes the whole process possible. We are joined to Him, and understanding that should not be relegated to "deep theology" which is never taught for fear it might be too deep for anyone to understand. This is where it begins, and the sooner the new convert understands this new position he or she is in, the better off they're going to be. Christians have a kind of split personality, and it can be enough to drive someone insane if they don't really understand that God resides within them, and is intertwined with them fundamentally and intimately.

Understanding this union with Him is key to understanding what Jesus meant when He said in John 15:4-7, "Remain in Me and I in you . . . without Me you can do nothing . . . If anyone doesn't remain in Me he dries up as a branch, they gather them together and throw them onto the fire where they are burned . . . If you remain in Me and My word remains in you, you will ask what you desire and it will be done for you." This is the sum total of the normal Christian life and experience. Draw closer to Him and do what He taught, and union with God is yours. Draw away from Him, and like a branch that has been cut off, you dry up and are eventually destroyed.

Sadly, the reason why most pastors don't preach on this subject is because they themselves don't understand it. It often doesn't fit within their theological framework, and so they don't know how to explain it to themselves, much less to their congregations. At other times, they don't understand how anything of a spiritual nature beyond the doctrine of justification could possibly be practical to their own lives, much less to anyone else's. Still others don't even try because it means that they'll have to give up things in their lives that they don't want to, or they know that it's not what people want to hear. For these latter pastors, they care more about keeping large congregations filling the tithe basket every Sunday than they do about feeding their sheep properly.

Fourth: of course, the death, burial, and resurrection of Jesus Christ. This is everything for the Christian. This is where we live, wrapped in His death, burial, and resurrection as we seek to express it within our own lives and beings.

Fifth: the practice of the faith. This is "What do we do?" as opposed to "What is it we are supposed to believe?" How do we draw closer to Him and embrace this union with Him? The old saying goes something like this, give a man a fish and he eats for a day, teach a man to fish and he eats for a lifetime. Why is it that we don't teach people what Christian practice, as Jesus and His Apostles taught it, looks like? Why is it that we're so often afraid of promoting the examples of people who actually did do what Jesus said to do? If we don't practice the faith, we can't draw closer to Him.

So, what is the practice of the faith? The practice of the faith is to move away from ourselves and towards Him. We do this through prayer, both in talking to God, and in listening to Him in stillness. We do this through voluntary poverty, giving up what we have to be free of the hold our possessions have on us. We do this through humility, keeping away from all thoughts of self-esteem. We also do this through self-control, not giving in to our desires to feel good. We choose to care about those who couldn't care less about us, and to defend those who can't defend themselves. We choose to do what He told us to do. *All* of what He told us to do.

Finally, the most important thing we can teach the new convert is the importance of love and compassion. It is more important than learning every doctrine perfectly, more important than tithing, more important than our own livelihoods or social standings or politics. It's more important than any Spiritual gift someone may or may not possess. Compassion doesn't judge. It doesn't retaliate. It forgives again and again and again. Love and compassion should be the absolute minimum of Christian faith and practice that is taught and displayed. It should be the thing that sets us apart from all others, the defining quality of the Christian faith. Compassion should be the first impression people get from a church, no matter which church it is. If someone doesn't understand that, then they don't understand Christ, the Gospel, or what it means to be Christian. If someone comes claiming to be a Christian but is without compassion or mercy, then that person is a liar and shouldn't even be given Holy Communion. It's that serious that we understand and practice Compassion.

These are the absolute fundamentals of the Christian faith. These are the basics that must be taught in order to lay a good foundation for the new Christian to build on. I agree that it's time to get back to the basics, and if we stick to the basics we'll make good progress. Yes, some of the other stuff is important too, but we can focus on that once we've mastered the basics.

7 | A Rant about the Job Description of Shepherds

I usually ramble. Right now, I want to rant. I feel like ranting and raving and making large gestures in the air with my hands and arms to the effect of "what the...? Are you kidding me? How can you... Ughhhhhh!" Yeah, something like that sounds about right.

I used to work in a children's home in a house full of teenage girls with emotional and psychological issues. It's not the only dorm on the campus, but it is the only one with girls in it. On Sundays, a group from a local church came in and set up shop to do services with the boys on campus who want to go, but nothing is made available for the girls. I was told that they used to do something for the girls, but they stopped when the number of girls interested dwindled to one, and the girls can't join the boys for services (for various, very legitimate reasons). The local church group felt that just one girl interested in services wasn't worth the effort. Thus my arm gesturing desire to rant and rave. Yes, the question comes up as to why I didn't just offer services to them, but the simple answer is that I was already staff, and by policy couldn't do anything that could be taken as proselytizing the residents. Cans of worms anyone?

I began to rant a little when I heard that, and one of my co-workers spoke up in the pastors' defense. She mentioned that maybe it didn't make much sense to them to just go and spend time doing a service for one girl when they could go and preach to hundreds. My response was "I'm going to shut up now," and I then went to go find something constructive to do while I bit my tongue, ranting in my head.

There is so much wrong with this kind of thinking towards pastoring that I don't even know where to begin to rant. As a priest, and thus as a pastor (which word literally means "shepherd"), my job is to give Jesus to people and be Jesus for people. This is the general job description of a shepherd of the Church. We feed the sheep. We keep the predators away. We tend the sick and injured, and we go after the ones that wander away from the rest of the flock. We put ourselves in harm's way to ensure the safety of the sheep. That is what we do. We spend long hours on hillsides watching and paying attention. We go sleepless at nights when one is being born. No one sheep is more important or less important than the others, and none of them are considered expendable. They don't belong to us, and each one is priceless to the Owner of the sheep.

We don't do this because it's fun. We do this because no shepherd belongs to himself. We ourselves are also the property of the Owner, and we are answerable to Him if one of the sheep is lost or injured because of our negligence. We don't get the excuse that, "Oh, it's just one sheep. She'll never be missed, and there are so many more." If you think I'm ranting about this kind of attitude, imagine how livid the Owner of the sheep is.

There's a story in *Eusebius' History of the Church* (Book III, xxiii: 6-19, 4th century, A.D.) about the Apostle John. I had originally thought to paraphrase it, but it really needs to be shared as it was written:

"Listen to a tale, which is not a mere tale, but a narrative concerning John the apostle, which has been handed down and treasured up in memory. For when, after the tyrant's death, he returned from the isle of Patmos to Ephesus, he went away upon their invitation to the neighboring territories of the Gentiles, to appoint bishops in some places, in other places to set in order whole churches, elsewhere to choose to the ministry some one of those that were pointed out by the Spirit.

"When he had come to one of the cities not far away (the name of which is given by some), and had consoled the brethren in other matters, he finally turned to the bishop that had been appointed, and seeing a youth of powerful physique, of pleasing appearance, and of ardent temperament, he said, 'This one I commit to you in all earnestness in the presence of the Church and with Christ as witness.' And when the bishop had accepted the charge and had promised all, he repeated the same injunction with an appeal to the same witnesses, and then departed for Ephesus.

"But the presbyter taking home the youth committed to him, reared, kept, cherished, and finally baptized him. After this he relaxed his stricter care and watchfulness, with the idea that in putting upon him the seal of the Lord he had given him a perfect protection.

"But some youths of his own age, idle and dissolute, and accustomed to evil practices, corrupted him when he was thus prematurely freed from restraint. At first they enticed him by costly entertainments; then, when they went forth at night for robbery, they took him with them, and finally they demanded that he should unite with them in some greater crime.

"He gradually became accustomed to such practices, and on account of the positiveness of his character, leaving the right path, and taking the bit in his teeth like a hard-mouthed and powerful horse, he rushed the more violently down into the depths. And finally despairing of salvation in God, he no longer meditated what was insignificant, but having committed some great crime, since he was now lost once for all, he expected to suffer a like fate with the rest. Taking them, therefore, and forming a band of robbers, he became a bold bandit-chief, the most violent, most bloody, most cruel of them all.

"Time passed, and some necessity having arisen, they sent for John. But he, when he had set in order the other matters on account of which he had come, said, 'Come, O bishop, restore us the deposit which both I and Christ committed to you, the church, over which you preside, being witness.'

"But the bishop was at first confounded, thinking that he was falsely charged in regard to money which he had not received, and he could neither believe the accusation respecting what he had not, nor could he disbelieve John. But when he said, 'I demand the young man and the soul of the brother,' the old man, groaning deeply and at the same time bursting into tears, said, 'He is dead.' 'How and what kind of death?' 'He is dead to God,' he said; 'for he turned wicked and abandoned, and at last a robber. And now, instead of the church, he haunts the mountain with a band like himself.'

"But the Apostle rent his clothes, and beating his head with great lamentation, he said, 'A fine guard I left for a brother's soul! But let a horse be brought me, and let some one show me the way.' He rode away from the church just as he was, and coming to the place, he was taken prisoner by the robbers' outpost. He, however, neither fled nor made entreaty, but cried out, 'For this did I come; lead me to your captain.'

"The latter, meanwhile, was waiting, armed as he was. But when he recognized John approaching, he turned in shame to flee. But John, forgetting his age, pursued him with all his might, crying out, 'Why, my son, do you flee from me, your own father, unarmed, aged? Pity me, my son; fear not; you have still hope of life. I will give account to Christ for you. If need be, I will willingly endure your death as the Lord suffered death for us. For you will I give up my life. Stand, believe; Christ has sent me.'

"And he, when he heard, first stopped and looked down; then he threw away his arms, and then trembled and wept bitterly. And when the old man approached, he embraced him, making confession with lamentations as he was able, baptizing himself a second time with tears, and concealing only his right hand.

"But John, pledging himself, and assuring him on oath that he would find forgiveness with the Saviour, besought him, fell upon his knees, kissed his right hand itself as if now purified by repentance, and led him back to the church. And making intercession for him with copious prayers, and struggling together with him in continual fastings, and subduing his mind by various utterances, he did not depart, as they say, until he had restored him to the church, furnishing a great example of true repentance and a great proof of regeneration, a trophy of a visible resurrection."

St. John the Apostle was paying attention when Jesus asked, "Which of you men, if you had one hundred sheep, and lost one of them, wouldn't leave the ninety-nine in the wilderness, and go after the one that was lost, until he found it?" (Luke 15:4, WEB)

Being a pastor has nothing to do with the size of your congregation. It doesn't matter if the Lord has entrusted to your care one, or a hundred and one. That person is still your responsibility. It doesn't matter if the sheep isn't being looked after by any one particular shepherd at the moment. That sheep belongs to the Owner and you are called and charged with looking after His sheep. Any and all of His sheep.

Someone might protest, "But that one's not a part of my flock, it's not my responsibility, it's that shepherd's over there. He needs to pay more attention." If you work for the Owner, and it's His sheep, it's your responsibility. Do you really want to have to explain why He lost some sheep when you could have prevented it?

I fear there are lost sheep for which I will likely have to answer. I honestly dread the day when I have to give an account of them because of my own negligence or ignorance. I won't sugar coat it. There are times when I really haven't known what to do, or have been too cowardly to do what I knew I should have. His sheep have paid the price. It terrifies me, as well it should. The Scriptures are clear on this also, that we who are teachers are held to a higher standard and a stricter judgment (James 3:1). In short, we claim to know better, and we claim to be able to teach others the Path of Jesus Christ. This knowledge we possess requires action. Just knowing this, by itself, terrifies me. Even if I should escape a reprimand, it doesn't mean everything is all right. His forgiving me doesn't change the consequences to the lost sheep.

Well, what if they have other responsibilities? What if it's too demanding on them? We are called first to love one another as He loved us. We are called to crucify ourselves, and put ourselves to death. Those of us who have been called to Ordination must be very careful to walk this path and not deviate from it. There is no other responsibility for us towards anyone, including ourselves, greater than crucifying ourselves and our own desires so that the life of Jesus Christ may be free flowing through us to all others around us.

If your "being Jesus" for someone has to take a back seat to some other priority, ditch the other priority. It's not worth it. Remember what He said to us, "inasmuch as you did it to one of the least of these my brothers, you did it to me." (Matthew 25:40, WEB) Those other priorities simply aren't worth treating our God and Savior with contempt because He's just one lone girl who might be interested in services on Sunday.

It doesn't matter if the congregation we preach to is hundreds of people or one person. We are called, as shepherds, to care for them. If you're one of the Rancher's shepherds and you see one of His sheep out by itself in the wild with no other shepherd in sight, it's your responsibility to look after it, not just let it go to fend for itself.

8 | A Ramble about an Ignored Passage

I ran across this passage the other night when I started reading back through 1 Corinthians again, and it's been stuck in my mind ever since:

1 Corinthians 5:9-13

"I wrote to you in my letter not to associate with sexually immoral people—not at all meaning the sexually immoral of this world, or the greedy and swindlers, or idolaters, since then you would need to go out of the world. But now I am writing to you not to associate with anyone who bears the name of brother if he is guilty of sexual immorality or greed, or is an idolater, reviler, drunkard, or swindler—not even to eat with such a one. For what have I to do with judging outsiders? Is it not those inside the church whom you are to judge? God judges those outside. 'Purge the evil person from among you.'" (ESV)

The more I think about it, the more I think this is probably one of the most ignored passages in scripture by professing Christians. What St. Paul is essentially saying is that we shouldn't be passing judgment on anyone outside of the Church. We simply don't have the right, and Jesus Himself said don't judge so that you won't be judged. But what he is also saying is that we have a responsibility to hold our brothers and sisters in Christ accountable for what they do and say, and correct them if they don't hold to the practice of the teaching of Jesus Christ. If they refuse to accept correction, then we are to purge them from the Church.

The truth is most churches and Christians that I have seen lately reverse this and practice the opposite, as though somehow St. Paul had it backwards. They thrive on holding outsiders accountable for not living according to Christian practices. They then say that we shouldn't judge or hold accountable our brothers and sisters who clearly either don't understand what Jesus taught, or simply don't care, and who don't believe they need do anything more than profess faith in Christ and show up at Church.

Those not joined to Christ through baptism are still blind spiritually, and have neither means nor inclination to follow Him. Thus, they have no ability to maintain a Christian standard of practice or ethics. How then could we possibly pass judgment on them? It really shouldn't matter who the non-believer is, or what religion, or to what philosophy they conform. What right do we have to revile them, bad-mouth them, or try to pressure them politically to conform to our standards and beliefs? Jesus went to their parties, healed them, exorcised their demons, and publicly defended them from the religious right of His day. He never humiliated them. He never mistreated them. He never turned any of them away.

Those who professed to know the truth however, to use a slang term, "He ripped a new one." His choice name for them was "sons of vipers." He spelled out every little thing they did wrong and called them on it in no uncertain terms. His chief complaint about them? Their utter lack of compassion, and their judgmentalism. In his stories, it was the sinful reject that cried out for mercy that was justified before God, not the self-professed saint who towed the religious line. He spent almost whole chapters in the Gospels saying "Woe to you scribes and Pharisees, hypocrites!"

How would Jesus treat the unbelieving woman who gets an abortion, or the doctor who performs it? How would He treat the Wiccan or Muslim who practices their faith? How would He treat the Christian who abuses them? What would He say to you or me? As Christians, we need to spend a lot less time praising ourselves for knowing the truth, and a lot more time doing it.

9 | A Ramble about Pulling Weeds

I was out watering my gardens this morning, as I do every morning. I skipped over the raspberry bushes because they're past bearing fruit at this point in time, and started on watering the bean plants I have in the back of the house.

These bean plants were an experiment of sorts. With our bean plants in the front, I carefully built rows and planted the seeds like I was taught in horticulture class in High School. With the plants in the back, instead of building rows with a hoe, I just scattered them over tilled soil to see if they would grow. When they didn't grow that way in the time it seemed like they should, we then decided to cover them over with mulch made from old grass clippings that smelled like horse manure. A few days later they sprouted aggressively, and they are now two or three times the size of the bean plants in the front.

As I watered, I began pulling some weeds that were obnoxiously big. It's my own fault that they got that way because I didn't pull them earlier when they were small, and, truth be told, I don't get out and weed as often as I should. So with the hose in one hand, I begin to use the other to get down to the base of the weed and yank it from the ground. The first one popped out without issue. Seeing my success, I go on to another. No problem. I then go on to the culprit that caught my attention to begin with.

I couldn't see the bottom of the plant because it was buried in among the bean plants. Trying to be as careful as I could I followed the stem of the weed with my hand, feeling it all the way down to the base of its stem. I then got my hand around it and pulled. Up it came . . .

Except it wasn't the weed that I had been trying to pull. It was a bean plant. It was a big, healthy bean plant with many seedpods on it that weren't quite mature, and blossoms which promised to turn into more seed pods. I looked at that weed with disgust, but I had no one else to blame but myself for the death of the bean plant. I was so intent on getting that weed, I had killed the plant I was trying to save instead.

One of the biggest problems with battling a false or heretical doctrine is that more often than not that heretical doctrine is wrapped around, or growing very close to, a very real and healthy faith in Jesus Christ accompanied with all the actions which underscore that faith. I remember one Mormon missionary I spoke to some time ago who told me his story. He had a girlfriend who was Baptist, and with whom he had a relationship which was quite serious. She came from a wealthy family, and he got along well with her family. The time came for him to go on his mission, and he was torn. He was told by both the girl and her family that if he chose to go on his mission for the LDS Church that it would be over between them. He told me that when it came down to it, He had to choose between Jesus Christ and his girlfriend. He chose Jesus Christ. This was a healthy plant regardless of the sizable weed, in my humble opinion, which was wrapped around it.

Jesus told a parable about wheat and weeds. He said:

"He put another parable before them, saying, 'The kingdom of heaven may be compared to a man who sowed good seed in his field, but while his men were sleeping, his enemy came and sowed weeds among the wheat and went away. So when the plants came up and bore grain, then the weeds appeared also. And the servants of the master of the house came and said to him, "Master, did you not sow good seed in your field? How then does it have weeds?" He said to them, "An enemy has done this." So the servants said to him, "Then do you want us to go and gather them?" But he said, "No, lest in gathering the weeds you root up the wheat along with them. Let both grow together until the harvest, and at harvest time I will tell the reapers, Gather the weeds first and bind them in bundles to be burned, but gather the wheat into my barn.""" (Matthew 13:24-30, ESV)

In context, as He explained it later, He was talking about people, and how the world, His field, would come to have both the sons of the evil one and the sons of the kingdom sown in it. But this passage has often come to my mind when thinking about all those people who believe something that has been regarded as heretical or false doctrine. We all accuse each other of this at some point in time. The Catholic labels the Protestant as heretical, the Protestant labels the Catholic as heretical, they both label the Mormon as heretical, and the Orthodox labels all of them as the much more polite term "heterodox." And we all seek to correct each other's dogmatic faults and bring them in line with our own. But in the process of doing so I have seen people walk away from Christ altogether, not knowing what to believe or why, because their faith was so integrally tied to their church and its dogmas. To my shame, I have been responsible for it at times.

The lesson of the bean plant tells me that sometimes it is better to leave the weed alone, however big and annoying it is, and let the plant you want flourish. Water it. Care for it. Isn't it better to tolerate a few weeds than to lose your harvest altogether?

Part VII | Reflections and Observations

1 | Rambling about Truth

H ave you ever come across something that disagrees with what you believe? It's a dumb question. Of course you have. Everyone has. Does it ever get to the point of threatening what you believe? Did you choose to outright reject it? Embrace it and overturn your belief? Or did you really wrestle with it and allow your faith to be strengthened and expanded without losing it altogether?

For those of us who profess faith in Jesus Christ, what is it that we are actually staking that faith on? A lot of times, I don't think we actually know what the foundation of our faith is, or is at least supposed to be, especially not at first. We are told it is about Jesus Christ, but then, as we are indoctrinated, the focus becomes on our political positions, our stands on creation, our stands on the end times, and various other minor theological doctrines. Often it seems that somewhere along the way of theological indoctrination, we forget what our faith was first based on.

I think in some ways that's what happened to me. When God first called me to come to Him, He called me as a Father to His long lost son. For me, He became a Father to this fatherless person (as I had felt during that time) that I had been. I didn't know anything about the Trinity. I didn't know really anything about man, sin, or salvation. All I knew was that He wanted to fill that place within me which had been empty for so long. He initiated that relationship, adopting this somewhat unwanted and misunderstood kid. Later on, I went through and became indoctrinated as to what it was I was supposed to believe and place my faith in, and then learned that I had done it all wrong. Bible School went further to make sure that I was properly saved, sealed, and delivered, according to the rules someone laid down somewhere, and that it was done in the "right" way.

And then I was thrown away, or at least it felt that way, by those guardians of that particular line of theology. They no longer had any use for me, and I was left adrift and disillusioned, wondering what I had done. I was then shown kindness by a different Church theology. And so I began to study that, and seemingly correct where I had been wrong before. But they placed limits on how useful I could be to God, supposedly, and He was telling me something different about those limits. And so, I began the study of yet another set of theologies. Each set of theologies were similar in so many ways, and yet it was the minute differences which built up the walls in between the people who championed them.

I'm being deliberately vague, although those who know my history know what I'm talking about, and those that don't might relate to it by filling in the blanks with their own experiences. Because in all of it, God has taught me that no matter how fine tuned and supposedly accurate or even Biblical a theological structure may be, it really doesn't matter.

What matters is Him. What matters is Jesus Christ. Jesus Christ was born, lived, taught, died, resurrected, and ascended two thousand years ago. There's enough evidence of the historical Jesus Christ that exists, direct and circumstantial, that the only people who don't accept this fact do so on blind faith. The Man was a real person in real history. When we say we're going to place our faith in Jesus Christ, then our faith needs to be grounded on these facts. When we say we're going to follow Him, then we need to sit down and study what He said and actually practice it. This is the whole idea of being a student. It's to learn from your teacher and be able to reproduce the practice or discipline that is taught in a real world setting. Jesus Christ and everything about Him is, and must be, the primary anchor of our faith. If the simple fact of His existence is not the foundation of your faith, than it will collapse under its own weight.

I see these as the anchors of my faith: the reality of Jesus Christ, my own personal experience and relationship with God (relationship being a two way street, by the way), the fact of my vows to follow Him, and my public commitment to do so by being baptized.

As for the rest of the theological wasteland we like to ramble around in . . . honestly, what difference does it make? How does it affect my practice of compassion and mercy as Jesus taught if I accept a six-day creation or theistic evolution? We're here. We weren't there when it happened. Get over it. How does it help me to not judge and to forgive if I am vehemently pre-tribulation rapture, mid-tribulation rapture, or post-tribulation rapture? The end will come whether we like it or not. He said so, and He didn't say when.

We get so worked up over so many theological minutiae that we actually violate what He taught in defending our own little beliefs. And when a set of data arrives that contradicts those little beliefs, we fall apart and lose our faith, or get angry and bash our brothers and sisters. I can't tell you how many times someone has questioned my salvation because I wore black clerics and a white collar. And yet those clothes symbolize my absolute devotion and service to our Lord.

Recently, as is my occasional practice, I translated in Matthew where the Pharisees were upset with Jesus' students over violating the tradition of the elders by eating with unwashed hands. He fired right back and accused them of violating a commandment of God because of one of their traditions. We are doing the same thing and transgressing the direct order and instruction of Jesus Christ when we place our own version of "truth" above compassion, love, and mercy upon our fellow brothers and sisters who profess faith in Him. And we blaspheme and shame Him to those who are outside the faith when we do this. Why would anyone want to be a "Christian" when we don't even follow Christ?

I'm ranting. I know. I want to see the Church restored to what He taught, and what He intended. That's not going to happen until we lose the theological baggage, our own "truth," and actually follow the One who *is* Truth. Our own "truth" is just another form of judgment and condemnation of others; "I'm right, and everyone else is wrong." It's narcissism dressed up in Sunday best, and it's self-centered at it's very core. Truth is compassion and mercy on the level that Jesus Christ taught and lived, praying for His enemies and forgiving them even as they were crucifying Him. This is Truth. This is the Faith. This is the example our Teacher set for us. This was His final and most important lesson before death.

2 | A Ramble about My Journey

Twenty years ago I called on God to be my Father and made the decision to take my Christianity seriously. I had little or no understanding of Christian doctrine then (I was fourteen). I just felt this irresistible pull towards God, and began reading the Scriptures and whatever books and materials I could get a hold of. At the time these were *The Book* (an edition of *The Living Bible*) and various books by Hal Lindsey.

I was a social outcast at the time. With an undiagnosed case of Asperger's syndrome, which no one at the time knew anything about, I barely understood my own feelings about anything. I really couldn't comprehend – and was unaware I couldn't comprehend – the experience of a basic relationship between two people. I was wrapped in my own world and withdrawn from the painful reality of the world of people around me. It was a world I didn't understand and had stopped trying to comprehend. Those decisions and choices weren't necessarily deliberate or conscious, but they were ones in which I was trapped nevertheless. This was the mental and emotional state I was in when I began to feel this pull.

One thing is for certain; I took it seriously. I have always taken it seriously. I took it seriously enough then to read everything I could about God, Christianity, and Christian practice. I began going to church voluntarily. This embroiled me in yet more relationships that I couldn't truly form with people that, by then, I had gone to school with and had known for several years, but hadn't seen for a while. It also embroiled me in relationships with people that didn't like me, and whom I knew didn't like me. I also knew that, in most cases, they had good reason not to.

So I continued learning everything that I could from sermons, the youth group, and other people at the church I attended. I tried to become more involved even though I was still deficient in knowing and understanding people. I thought I knew what Christianity was all about from the sermons, the books, the people, and the Bible itself.

I then had the privilege of going on a missions trip overseas to Papua New Guinea. This trip taught me lessons that I continue to look back on to this day. It was the first time, as I returned from New Guinea, that my eyes were really opened to the fact that something wasn't quite right with the Church. Learning all the "right" doctrines, going to church on Sundays, and doing all the things with the church youth group: these were all good things, but somehow the whole "environment" was still missing something. At the time I just thought it was a lack of devotion or a lack of willingness to put everything on the line, like the missionaries with whom I had just spent two months did. It was an illusion that wasn't dispelled even later on, when I went to a Bible school run by the same missions organization. I spent two more years with that organization. If nothing else they tried to reinforce the illusion, consciously or not.

It was during these earliest times in my own journey of faith when I was struck with the simple, inexplicable fact that the Christians, the churches, the books, and I myself were all missing something; something important in our faith and the way we lived our lives. I had no idea what it could be when I started, and still very little idea when I made the first realization of it. But I spent the next fifteen years after that first Bible school trying to find what was missing, believing that I had, then realizing that I hadn't found anything. I saw glimmers of it every now and then, like pieces of a puzzle that someone has scattered around a house and then left for someone else to pick up.

I read book after book. Some were profoundly worthwhile; others were little more than fluff, while yet others had no right to call themselves Christian. For a time I even read works outside of the Christian tradition and gained some insights that drove me straight back to the Scriptures and Christ Himself. By the grace of God I was driven towards the ancient roots of the faith, and the rich body of writings and Tradition left by those who lived within a few generations of the Apostles. These followers of Christ knew what the Apostles, and Christ Himself, taught far better than we do today. I continued to be pulled irresistibly towards God and to seek the answer as to what was missing.

I searched ancient Church Fathers and masters of the faith of Jesus Christ, and these led me to delve even further into a place of prayer that, not long before, I had no idea even existed. I have attempted to seek the holy darkness, the void where there is only God, and have been frustrated and confused when I couldn't, when just the day before I had experienced a wonder in prayer to where I had no desire to leave. I fought, and continue to struggle within myself over the most benign of actions or ways to spend my time.

And twenty years later, humbly, I have come to the conclusion that what is called "Christian" today is often not, neither do many who use the word have any understanding of it means. I have come to the conclusion that I am often not Christian in my thoughts, my words, or my actions. I look back on those who came before us, many hundreds of years ago; I read their words and what they knew and experienced, and I know that I am nothing in comparison. What is far, far worse than this is that we have so carelessly twisted and abused the faith which those ancient Fathers of the Faith gave their whole lives, and their deaths, to pass down to us, that it now resembles little more than a caricature.

Christianity isn't a set of doctrines. It's a practice and a discipline and an agreement with God that you will cooperate with Him through renouncing yourself, your possessions, your wants, and even your bodily appetites in the pursuit of experiencing the one relationship that truly matters more than anything else. It's regarding your favorite TV show, the things you're proud of accomplishing, and your prized book collection as little more than trash in the active pursuit of knowing and drawing close to Him. It's taking a hard, honest look at yourself and admitting to yourself that death is only a breath away, and that if you were to stand in judgment, it would be absolutely damning. It's realizing that it is only because God loves you and because of His mercy that you have not been destroyed already, and that He is capable and willing to deliver even you for the sake of Jesus Christ. Christianity is letting go of everything that we have done or been before and reaching ahead towards Him, not looking back.

Christianity is a constant fight with your innermost desires and thoughts, and the constant whispers of unclean spirits in your ears seeking to either puff you up with pride or drag you down in despair. They whisper in quiet voices for you to do anything other than to walk the razor sharp line in between pride and despair, which is humility, an honest appraisal of yourself, and acceptance of the love of God. Christianity is the fight to leave off eating until you spend time in prayer in the morning, or to spend time in contemplation of God instead of watching science fiction re-runs. It's the hard work of emptying yourself, emptying your mind in the hopes of brushing up against the holy darkness of His presence. It's also having to walk away without what you sought, because He doesn't want you to harm yourself spiritually, being destroyed by pride, because He gave you more than you're capable of just yet. It's the never ending battle against yourself, your own laziness, your own lack of empathy, your own ignorance, weakness, blindness, and your own refusal to admit these things.

Christianity is the embrace of suffering; any and all suffering which destroys and breaks down the ego for the sake of Jesus Christ. It's the deliberate choice to tell yourself "no" to even the most benign of distractions that come between you and your Lord. It is the Cross of Jesus Christ and the embrace of it into our lives until it burns its way down deep into us, and we ourselves are destroyed and out of the way. It is destroying our own psyche in order to deliver it. It is dying that He might live within, and that He would live His life out through us. It is the hard work of building that relationship through Jesus Christ between you and God and defending that relationship at all costs as more important than your possessions, your comforts, all other relationships, and your very life.

What's most often missing in the churches today is not some doctrine or study or "new" idea. There is a seemingly endless supply of those. What's missing most often in the churches today is a very old idea that the ancient fathers of the Church understood only too well. What's missing is Christianity itself.

3 | A Ramble about Divorce

My family history is complicated. I was thinking about it last night as my wife and I were talking. In a very real way I am a product of divorce, and in more than one way.

My maternal biological grandfather was married once before my grandmother. To my knowledge, that first marriage ended in divorce (although I don't know the circumstances) and he married my grandmother. He later died at the end of World War II when my grandmother was still pregnant with my mother. My paternal grandmother was married twice. To my knowledge, her first marriage ended in divorce, and my grandmother later married my paternal grandfather. My father was born and around ten years later my grandfather divorced my grandmother and moved across the country. My parents divorced when I was seven. Both of my sisters have gone through divorces. The impact of these events on our family, among other things, shaped it into the state it is in today.

Divorce is an ugly thing. Truth is, I can't even comprehend separating from my wife under those circumstances. She's such a part of who I am it would be like ripping away the best part of myself. I would be horribly incomplete without her, and to imagine it under those circumstances is, well . . . unimaginable.

Divorce is painful to everyone going through it, and it has a ripple effect that radiates outward. But it does happen. Sometimes, as much as many would like to deny it possible, there are very good reasons for it. Sometimes, as much as some would like to deny it, there aren't. There is an opinion within some quarters of the Church that somehow divorced people are "less than," irredeemable, or second class citizens. In some churches they are forbidden from entering the clergy, in others they are forbidden from taking communion, and in still others are simply discussed behind their backs.

Another person in my life who has been divorced is God. Sound surprising? It surprised me too when a pastor I know brought it up years ago when I was sitting in his congregation. But the Holy Scriptures are clear on this. God Himself says it:

"Thus says Yahweh, 'Where is the bill of your mother's divorce, with which I have put her away? Or which of my creditors is it to whom I have sold you? Behold, for your iniquities were you sold, and for your transgressions was your mother put away.'" (Isaiah 50:1, WEB)

"Contend with your mother! Contend, for she is not my wife, neither am I her husband; and let her put away her prostitution from her face, and her adulteries from between her breasts;" (Hosea 2:2, WEB)

"I saw, when, for this very cause that backsliding Israel had committed adultery, I had put her away and given her a bill of divorce, yet treacherous Judah, her sister, didn't fear; but she also went and played the prostitute." (Jeremiah 3:8, WEB)

It was a bitter, ugly, nasty divorce that is spelled out in all it's gory detail over the pages of the Old Testament prophets. He hates divorce, yes. But I imagine anyone who's been through it shares the same sentiment and never wants to repeat the experience. In some churches, God Himself would be excommunicated, forbidden from ministry, or talked about in the back pews in whispers.

It's never a good thing to pass judgment on someone for being divorced (or anything else for that matter). We may not like the actions taken, but I imagine that we would like it even less if we were in their shoes and being presented with the same choices. Maybe we would make the same decisions. Maybe we wouldn't. Maybe we really don't want to be in a position to find out.

As I reflected back on the divorces in my family, I realized that if they hadn't occurred then I wouldn't have been born. Neither would my children have been born. I can't ever characterize a divorce as a "good" thing. But sometimes, bad things have to happen in order for good things to grow. When things decay and die they fertilize soil and provide food for plants to grow in. Sometimes they fertilize weeds and thorns. Sometimes they fertilize flowers and fruit trees. It depends on how you manage the ground it fertilizes. People die. Relationships die. One's beliefs and faith sometimes die. One's hopes for the future or ties to the past also die. These things decay, and we have to work with the ground they fertilize.

4 | A Ramble about Failure

Some time ago I watched a movie called *Meet the Robinsons*, and in it there is one scene which stands out in particular. The main character, a boy with a knack for invention, attempts to fix an automatic peanut butter and jelly squirter designed to dispense just the right amount of peanut butter and jelly onto two slices of bread. He does his best at it, and then tries to operate the machine . . . which fails spectacularly in front of a large family that has been kind to him. He feels frustrated and embarrassed, but then they turn to him and start extolling the virtues of failure (singing about it unless I'm mistaken) with excited gusto.

We don't prize failure. I can't think of any culture (except the fictional Robinsons) that does. Failures are worthless, and are to be pushed aside by those who can show that they succeed. Failures make no one proud, especially when it's repetitive. Sooner or later, the people who make them are told to just give up.

Being a failure doesn't take much. You just have to make a mistake at the wrong time. Often the only difference between success and failure is chance, stress, or the wrong thought at the wrong time. Failure happens to everyone, but few will choose to admit it and even fewer will choose to take responsibility for it. It is always the fault of someone or something else.

Most people would consider me a failure, for various reasons. There are some days when I don't disagree. I make mistakes. Those mistakes have consequences to them. I could argue about whether or not those consequences are fair, but since when has life been fair? I didn't graduate High School. When I did go to college, my chosen major was one that is nearly impossible to make money at (and is often looked at as underwater basket weaving). I've had more (paying) jobs over the last twelve years then I care to think about. My family and I almost always seem to be in challenging situations, and it gets tiresome very quickly. Much of this has been due to choices (good, bad, or somewhere in-between) that I've made. Some of it has been due to other people making choices that have affected my family and I. And some of it has been things that happened out of the blue that required me to make choices I didn't expect to have to make, and we then had to ride out the storm that followed.

Failures, however, are first about learning opportunities. You find out what you did wrong, and then you find a solution to the problem. This is an easy enough philosophy to implement when you are talking about experimentation and invention, but it becomes more complicated when you're talking about choices that are made with things that affect your life, and others as well. Failures can still be learning opportunities, but they are exponentially harder to recover from.

Second, failures aren't always what they seem to be. A failure generally means that something happened which you didn't intend. But all too often, this doesn't mean something bad. Just because you didn't intend for it, and the resulting consequences, to happen doesn't make it wrong or a bad thing for you. Often it means an open door in a direction you didn't know about when you started.

When I look back over my life I see all the failures that I've accumulated over the years, and all the different directions which those failures have taken me. Those failures eventually led to my getting married and having a family when it was statistically improbable for me. Those failures also led me into ministry and ordination. Some of those failures allowed my family and I a couple of years of peace and stability, others allowed me to co-pastor a parish. Still others allowed me to receive treatment and to beat a disorder which few if any others in the world have been able to beat. It was more often than not my failures that opened up these doors, not my successes.

As I sit here rambling and contemplating my latest failure, I do regret it. There are real consequences that have followed and will follow that not only affect my family and I, but also will affect others. There's nothing I can do now to stop that chain of events from unfolding in whatever way it will. But if my experience at being a failure tells me anything at all, it tells me that, far from only being negative, this failure will also open up possibilities that were otherwise not possible.

5 | Rambling about Reincarnation

I worked in the receiving department at a local "big box store" for over a year and a half. Since well before I had been hired, the department had been considered well below the productivity standards that the corporate powers that be wanted. According to our managers, our department wasn't accomplishing what it was supposed to. Don't get me wrong, I and the other unloaders worked hard, really hard, fighting to get the freight unloaded and out to the sales floor in time to be stocked by the next shift of stockers. But somehow we never quite seemed to make the cut.

The standard management response to this continued under-performance was to locate the problem employees and weed them out, replacing them with employees who would, or at least might, perform according to expectations.

In over a year and a half, I was the sole unloader left from the original receiving team when I was hired. The average size of a team was supposed to be eight people on any given night. The average length of service in the receiving department was about 4 or 5 months. In the time I had been there, we had undergone a complete turnover in personnel. We had changed supervisors three or four times. We had four or five Assistant Store Managers in succession overseeing the loading dock, and we had two Store Managers at the store's helm.

I reflected on this, because the under-performance continued seemingly uninterrupted. The internal problems, complaints, and attitudes were exactly the same as when I had been hired. The grievances between employee and manager continued to be identical, and yet it wasn't the same set of people.

It got me thinking. We weren't the same set of people at all, and yet in some ways we were. We had our own lives, our own personalities, our own sets of strengths and weaknesses, and yet we continued to perpetuate the same cycles of performance as those who came before us. It is likely that after I left that store, it continued on without interruption.

We do tend to carry on the ideas, attitudes, and ways of thinking of those that came before us whether we're conscious of them or not. When someone who is racist has a child, and they teach that child racism and hatred, that child, if he does not choose a different path, continues that cycle of racism and hatred. It becomes re-incarnated from parent to child or teacher to student. Racism is just one obvious example, but there are other things that get passed on. Some of them, like prejudice, are harmful. Some of them, like ways of dressing or speaking, are benign. Still others, like faith and compassion, are beneficial. But they get passed on and re-incarnate into the next generation, just like the attitudes and ways of thinking have re-incarnated from unloader to unloader and manager to manager.

The psyche is unique to each individual; being a combination of the material and immaterial parts of the human being, just as each physical body and life experience is unique to each individual. It does not and really cannot transmigrate. But we do suffer the consequences of the thoughts and actions of those who come before us as they transmit them to us, either by taking on their suffering and ignorance, or by reaping the benefits of their blessing and enlightenment. At times, it is a mixture of both.

The word "reincarnate" means "to take up flesh again," or "to be re-embodied." As I look at my children and interact with them, I see myself and my wife in them as well. We are reincarnated in our children as we pass on our traits, physical and psychological, natural and learned, to them. At times, it's like looking in a mirror, and yet they are themselves; unique individuals all three of them. My children both suffer for and reap the benefits of the consequences of our thoughts and actions as well. They do so more acutely than anyone else I come into contact with.

In this we also have choices to make, and we *can* make choices to move past our generational and experiential programming. These are hard choices to make, but they can be made. My son can make the choice to react as I do to different circumstances, or he can choose a different path if he is willing and able to see it.

The choice to be a Christian is the choice to allow a single Person to override all of our physical and experiential programming and to re-incarnate Himself into us, with His traits imprinted over ours, with everything that He is being reborn into us. The scripture says,

"For you died, and your life is hidden with Christ in God." (Colossians 3:3, WEB)

Everything which came before us and reincarnated itself into us suddenly has a death certificate signed on it, and the only real input that matters is that of Jesus Christ.

But this reincarnation takes place upon a choice that we must make on a decision by decision basis. Do we continue to dwell in our own selves, the combinations of biology and experiences which form who we consider ourselves to be, or do we abandon this self to death, pursuing Jesus Christ and who He is?

We know that this self, one way or another, will end in death. This is unavoidable. We know that those who have been baptized into Christ Jesus have been joined to His death and died with Him already, so that when this person physically dies, it is no great loss. It is only the finalization of what already is. And, as we were joined with Him in His death, so we are also joined with Him in His resurrection. His thoughts, actions, and who He is overrides who we are or were, as the case may be. He breaks the cycle as we are united to a single, immortal Being.

With this in mind, it could be said that the true Christian life is the practice of re-incarnation, as we choose to practice the re-incarnation of Jesus Christ in us.

6 | A Ramble about Judgment Day

The most just judgment anyone can receive is the consequence of their own actions. It isn't always the most merciful, but in terms of justice or fairness you can't get more fair than making a person lie down in the bed they made for themselves. More often than not, those consequences affect other people as well. They tend to have a ripple effect and pass from person to person, and often people halfway around the world that you don't know can be affected through a chain of consequences begun by you.

Actions that are kind, caring, and beneficial to other people will almost always have good consequences for everyone involved, even if you can't see them in that moment. Actions that are selfish, self-centered, and harmful will always have bad consequences for everyone involved, and often for many people who had nothing to do with it. You may not see them right away, but they manifest themselves eventually. Sometimes, the longer those consequences take to manifest, the more potent they are.

You know it's not good when watching the evening news resembles a cheesy b-rated end times movie, or book for that matter (I ought to know, I read enough of them in my younger days). I also read a lot of Hal Lindsey when I was a teenager, and he was probably my first introduction to Christian discipleship and theology. Needless to say, I disagree with a lot of what he had to say then. But there is one salient point, his major point, which I am coming to agree with more and more. Judgment Day isn't just coming; it's either extremely near, or else we're in the beginning stages of it.

No, I'm not basing this opinion on the moral state of the world, neither am I basing it on the current political situation in the Middle East. I am also not basing it on some book I've read. What's more, I think most people can sense it as well.

Do I think that God is finally venting His anger on us? Honestly . . . no. I don't think this has anything to do with God's anger. I think this is God allowing us, as a species, to reap a sometimes literal whirlwind of our own actions.

Tonight on the news they reported that food prices, globally, are about to skyrocket. This has been caused by bad harvests. Those bad harvests have been due to the devastating weather patterns we've now been having for the last year or two. Whole crops have been destroyed. There are now very few credible scientists who believe that these weather events aren't either caused or influenced by human induced global warming. This human induced global warming is caused, in large part, by the technological advances (and widespread usage of that technology) made in the last three hundred years. The impetus for those technological advances, in almost every case, was to help people live longer and so that they don't have to work hard, or at least not as hard as they used to (relatively speaking, given when the individual tech advance was made).

So we can boil down just the disastrous weather events and the food shortages which have been happening to two primary causes. The first is to stave off death as long as possible. The second is to keep from working hard. Remember Genesis 3? What consequence did God give Adam (which could also be translated as "Mankind") specifically? To paraphrase, "You will work really hard scratching a living from the soil, and you will die." So, the impetus for all of our technological advances can really be boiled down to the refusal to accept what God decided for us to begin with. And this refusal has literally condemned mankind, and every other creature on Earth.

We can also trace a number of contributing factors in the same manner back to desires to feel good, desires to have more, and desires to become something more or believe we are something more than we are. This can be traced back, not to just a few isolated individuals, but to humanity as a whole. Greed, for example, is the desire to have more than you already do. This is what drives corporate executives. Those same corporate executives then make decisions about which course of action will make them the most money with as little risk to themselves as possible. These kinds of decisions are what drove the Deep Water Horizon disaster in the Gulf of Mexico, and drive oil companies to strangle any alternative fuel research they can. These kinds of decisions are what drove the recent financial crises, and continue to drive US unemployment as more jobs are shipped overseas (which is why the recession has technically ended even though huge numbers of people are out of work). Think it through and you will see that all of these things can be traced back to someone, somewhere, acting selfishly to any degree on one of these desires.

From a certain point of view, mankind is in fact being judged for our refusal to obey the Gospel. Not it's refusal necessarily to believe the Gospel, but to obey it. What do I mean by this? The Gospel of Jesus Christ, as most Bible school professors will teach, is that Jesus Christ died for our sins according to the Scriptures. That He was buried, and that He was raised the third day according to the Scriptures. According to most census figures, at least half the planet believes this in one way or the other.

But is this really all that it is? No. The Gospel of Jesus Christ is Jesus Christ Himself. It is everything about Him. He is the Teaching. His life, His death, and His resurrection are all a part of the Gospel. The Gospel is the cross as well as the resurrection. The Teaching of Jesus Christ was and is, essentially, a life of poverty, self-control, and humility. If we all obeyed the Cross, denying ourselves and picking it up like He told us to, then this world wouldn't be in the position it's in right now.

If we all abandoned our desires to have more stuff, if we all abandoned our desires to feel good and not work hard, if we all abandoned our fear of death (which is meaningless for those in Christ Jesus) and embraced it when He chooses for it to happen, if we all were truly honest with ourselves and with life and exercised those simple constraints which He Himself practiced and taught, then none of these disastrous things which have happened recently would have happened.

But this isn't a judgment on a single individual, or even everyone individually. This is a judgment on mankind as a whole as it reaps the consequences of its choices throughout thousands of years of human history. No one individual can take full responsibility for all of it. We all share in it, we all have a part. And just as it took more than one person to bring it about, it will take all of humanity making really hard choices, which it doesn't want to make, to stop this process before it gets worse; if it can be stopped at all. We may already be past the point of no return weather wise, if some scientists quoted in the news can be believed.

This is why, unfortunately, it won't stop. Mankind as a whole doesn't want to make those choices. Mankind as a whole wants more stuff. Mankind wants the easy life. Mankind doesn't care whom it has to hurt to get it. Mankind wants to live as long as possible because it's terrified of death. Mankind wants to feel good.

I wish I were wrong. This is my opinion, and only my opinion, on the state of the world right now. If things suddenly turn around and get better, I'll be the first one to admit that I was wrong and give a huge sigh of relief. I wish that this wasn't a giant mirror that we as a species are being forced to look at to show us what we truly are, but it is. That's why He allows us to suffer the consequences of our actions, so that we take a good hard look at ourselves and make the choice to change our hearts and minds and repent, but a collective malfunction requires a collective repair.

I wish that somehow we could all be "raptured" away from what's about to happen, but that was never the teaching of the ancient Church. They understood that we would all go through the fire together and come out the other side with all of our gooses at least a little cooked, and that we who follow Jesus Christ would need to continue to do so until the end no matter what happened.

So, we have global weather disasters, global food shortages, global unemployment, we know that oil will run dry within the next fifty years (some analysts saying twenty), and riots and revolutions. One CIA analysis released a couple of years ago, and quoted in the news, said that these are their primary areas of concern regarding potential near future conflicts and wars. The scariest thing of all is that it's likely to be only the beginning.

I think most people sense it somewhere inside themselves. Some kind of Judgment Day is upon us, and it is the consequences of our own actions that are judging us. I truly hope our Lord Jesus Christ does come back soon, otherwise there won't be anyone left after we're done with ourselves.

7 | A Ramble about Counseling

I've done a fair amount of counseling over the last twenty years. Oddly enough, I've never really been a professional counselor. I've never really gotten paid for it, and it always seems to happen when I least expect it, in just those right moments. Near as I can tell, it's my own peculiar "charism," otherwise known as a spiritual gift. I know it's not a natural one, because every time I've found myself in a counseling situation thinking I was prepared and could handle it, I couldn't have been more wrong. Those situations still make me twitch when I think about them.

I've never been naturally suited to counseling, but it's never really been much of a choice for me either. It happens in those moments when Grace takes over and says "Sit down, buckle up, shut your mouth, and hold on!" It started when I was in high school, and over the years I've learned more and more to keep my proverbial mouth shut even as I hear words and ideas flowing from my literal mouth that weren't my own thoughts to begin with. I also begin to know, understand, and see things about the person that I couldn't possibly have known, and often don't remember after the fact. More often than not, I learn just as much from what comes out of my mouth as the person I'm counseling does, and I wish I could remember more of it.

In any given counseling situation, I've learned more and more to say less and less. The best thing I can do, as those situations have taught me, is to say nothing and just listen as well as I can. I've often heard that you need to take the person where they're at. As I've been around and near more professional counselors in the last few years, I've made the observation that that is too simplistic of a way to put it.

There are three ways to take someone where they're at: 1) where the person believes himself to be at, 2) where you, the counselor, believe the person to be at, and 3) where the person is actually at. It complicates it further in that each interaction between two or more people changes each person in either a large or small way, so that where they were at prior to speaking to you is different from where they are at while they are speaking to you. This is also different from where they are at after speaking to you. It's much like trying to measure both the speed and the position of a sub-atomic particle. You can measure the speed accurately, or you can measure the position accurately, but never both, because just the fact you are trying to measure it changes the measurement. People are much the same way.

I found the best way to gauge a person is to say nothing, give no input, and just let them talk. Let them tell you where they're at. After they do so, make no judgments about where they think they're at. Most often, I've come to realize, there's absolutely nothing I can say that can actually make a person see things the way I do. I've argued my case before. I've tried to persuade. It never works, especially if a person is convinced that they are a certain way and life is a certain way. More often then not, attempts to persuade only cause the person to reinforce their own view of things against the view I am trying to superimpose.

The person you are trying to counsel is never going to be coming from the same place you are at. They may be coming from similar places; they may have had similar experiences. But they are not you. Attempting to approach them with "common sense" almost always fails, because common sense is relative to the person who believes it should be common.

In many ways, the person we are now is made up of the experiences we have had from birth, as well as the choices to which those experiences have led. No one, from creation until now, has had the exact same set of experiences. No one has the exact same brain chemistry. No one makes their choices in exactly the same manner.

I often get the sense as I watch other people giving counsel that, as they initially begin to listen to the person, they know or believe they know where the person is actually at, even if the person is telling them something completely different from the counselor's conclusion. While it is true that counselors often get told about a reality that doesn't exist, it is equally true that such a reality often exists in that person's mind and is how they are perceiving the world. In such a case it occurs to me that the perceived reality must be really listened to and taken into serious consideration when giving counsel, even if the counselor does not perceive it as reality.

Often, what any one person perceives as reality is very different from what another person perceives as reality. This is why we have Republicans and Democrats, Christians and Buddhists, Creationists and Evolutionists, and so on. This is why we have so many differing points of view, because the experiences and choices that we have made and encountered have "programmed" us to perceive reality in different and opposing ways, even if it is the same reality we are perceiving.

All too often, it seems to me, counseling is used as a tool to try and get the other person to see things the way the counselor sees them, because, of course, the counselor sees them in the "right way." Or, the counselor is the one in his "right mind." All too often, the counseling session is used to pass judgment on the other person's perception of reality.

It is true that one person's perception of reality may lead that person into harming themselves or others. Do we intervene then? Are they really causing harm to themselves or another person? What is the rule to go by in deciding whether or not to intervene, and who's to say we're right in doing so? These are all questions, I think, which really need to be contemplated.

Ultimately, the only one who can really change a person's life is that person himself. Others would argue here that God is the one who changes lives. Again, it is a matter of perception. God goes out of His way to arrange our experiences in such a way to where we will make the choices He favors as healthy ones (as He is the only One qualified to decide what Reality actually is, and where a person is actually at). But when it comes right down to it, we still have to make those choices. God can throw everything at a person imaginable. He can rain Grace down on that person in unimaginable torrents. But that person still has to make the choice to go this way or that. God won't do it for him. Even if He's capable of forcing him to choose one or the other, He still won't do it. It's that person's choice to continue to accept his perceived reality or to allow a change in that perceived reality towards that which God is telling that person is Reality.

I have become convinced that there is nothing I can say or do with a person which will change their life. Nor should I ever dupe myself into thinking that I can (sadly, I've done just that before; it wasn't pretty). My interaction with them might cause a change in direction, as all interactions must, but the person must make those choices for themselves. It must be their choice whether they decide life is fair or unfair. It's their choice to decide whether they're ugly or pretty, smart or stupid, or priceless or worthless, and they will decide this based on their experiences both old and new, long past and recent, including the conversation they hold with me, whether I say anything or not.

Sources Mentioned or Cited

Print:

Anonymous. *The Cloud of Unknowing.* Bernard Bangley, ed. & trans. Brewster, MA: Paraclete Press, 2006. Print.

A Dictionary of Early Christian Beliefs. Bercot, David W. ed. Peabody, MA: Hendrickson Publishers, 1998. Print.

The Gospel of Buddha. Carus, Paul, ed. Chicago and La Salle, IL: Open Court, 1894 (1990). Print.

Tzu, Lao. *Tao Te Ching.* Mair, Victor H., trans. New York: Quality Paperback Book Club, 1998.

The Philokalia, Vol. I. Palmer, G.E.H, Philip Sherrard, and Kallistos Ware, trans. and ed. New York: Faber and Faber, 1979. Print.

The Philokalia, Vol. II. Palmer, G.E.H, Philip Sherrard, and Kallistos Ware, trans. and ed. New York: Faber and Faber, 1981. Print.

The Philokalia, Vol III. Palmer, G.E.H, Philip Sherrard, and Kallistos Ware, trans. and ed. New York: Faber and Faber, 1984. Print.

The Philokalia, Vol. IV. Palmer, G.E.H, Philip Sherrard, and Kallistos Ware, trans. and ed. New York: Faber and Faber, 1995. Print.

Parker, Robert Christopher Townley. "sacrifice, Greek." *The Oxford Companion to Classical Civilization.* Hornblower, Simon and Anthony Spawforth, ed. New York: Oxford University Press, 1998. Print.

Plato. *The Republic*. Lee, Desmond, trans. New York: Penguin Books, 1955.

Ross, Hugh. *The Creator and the Cosmos*. Colorado Springs: Navpress, 1993.

Ross, Hugh. *The Fingerprint of God*. Orange, Calif.: Promise Publishing Co., 1989.

Ware, Kallistos. *The Orthodox Way, rev. ed*. Crestwood, NY: St. Vladimir's Seminary Press, 1998. Print.

Electronic Sources:

"Divinization (Christian)." *Wikipedia.org.* http://en.wikipedia.org/wiki/Theosis. Website.

"Prime Directive." *Wikipedia.org.* http://en.wikipedia.org/wiki/Prime_Directive. Website.

The Paradise of the Desert Fathers. http://www.coptic.net/articles/ParadiseOfDesertFathers.txt. Website.

The Sayings of the Desert Fathers. http://www.coptic.net/articles/SayingsOfDesertFathers.txt. Website.

Pamphilus, Eusebius. "Church History." McGiffert, Arthur Cushman, trans. *Nicene and Post-Nicene Fathers, Second Series, Vol. 1. Schaff, Philip and Henry Wace, ed.* Buffalo, NY: Christian Literature Publishing Co., 1890. Revised and edited for New Advent by Kevin Knight. http://www.newadvent.org/fathers/250103.htm. Website.

Television and Films:

"Rightful Heir." *Star Trek: The Next Generation*. UPN, 17 May, 1993. Television.

Anderson, Steve, dir. *Meet the Robinsons*. Walt Disney Pictures, 2007. Film.

Avildsen, John G, dir. *The Karate Kid*. Columbia Pictures, 1984. Film.

Bertolucci, Bernardo, dir. *Little Buddha*. Miramax Films, 1994. Film.

Cain, Christopher, dir. *The Next Karate Kid*. Columbia Pictures, 1994. Film.

Columbus, Chris, dir. *The Bicentennial Man*. Touchstone Pictures, 1999. Film.

Lucas, George, dir. Star Wars Episode II: The Attack of the Clones. Twentieth Century Fox, 2002. Film.

Lucas, George, dir. *Star Wars Episode IV: A New Hope*. Twentieth Century Fox, 1977. Film.

Lucas, George, dir. *Star Wars Episode V: The Empire Strikes Back*. Twentieth Century Fox, 1980. Film.

Wachowski, Larry, and Andy Wachowski, dir. *Matrix*. Warner Bros. Pictures, 1999. Film.

Zwart, Harald, dir. *The Karate Kid*. Columbia Pictures, 2010. Film

Music:

Jackson, Michael. *Man in the Mirror*. Epic, 1988. Song.

Gaga, Lady. *Judas*. Streamline, 2011. Song.